Little Billy's Letters

The author when he was around Little Billy's age.

Little Billy's Letters

[An Incorrigible Inner Child's Correspondence with the Famous, Infamous, and Just Plain Bewildered]

Bill Geerhart

HARPER

NEW YORK · LONDON · TORONTO · SYDNEY

HARPER

A hardcover edition of this book was published in 2010 by William Morrow, an imprint of HarperCollins Publishers.

Some of these letters have previously appeared in *Radar* magazine.

Desert Storm and Enduring Freedom trading cards © Topps.

HarperCollins books may be purchased for educational, business, or sales promotional use. For information please write: Special Markets Department, HarperCollins Publishers, 10 East 53rd Street, New York, NY 10022.

FIRST HARPER paperback published 2011.

Designed by Richard Oriolo

The Library of Congress has catalogued the hardcover editon as follows:

Geerhart, Bill.
    Little Billy's letters : an incorrigible inner child's correspondence with the famous, infamous, and just plain bewildered / Bill Geerhart. —1st ed.
        p. cm.
    ISBN 978-0-06-180728-2
    1. Celebrities—Humor. 2. Politicians—Humor. 3. American wit and humor. I. Title.

    PN6231.C25G44 2010.
    818'.602—dc22

                                                    2009033146

ISBN 978-0-06-201510-5 (pbk.)

11 12 13 14 15   OV/RRD   10 9 8 7 6 5 4 3 2 1

My brother Chuck, sister Connie, me, and Tippy the Dog.

For Connie Geerhart, a little sister who has put up with way too much

pe used to sen
If this is true I
her back to the
Dinosores. How mu
cost? Please wr
back!

Than

Billy

[CONTENTS]

Dear Mr. Linkletter,
I am thinking of dropping out
of school. My uncle said I
should write to you. What
do you think of my plans?
please allso send me a picture.
                    Thanks,
                    Billy

[INTRODUCTION]

"Getting a letter made you feel like you were part of something bigger than yourself."

—Kevin Costner as a postapocalyptic mail carrier in the 1997 flop, *The Postman*

"We advise our clients not to send personal responses to their fans. The only exception might be for a critically ill child."

—Jeff Marquart of Gavin de Becker & Associates, a firm that specializes in threat assessment, as quoted in "Walter Scott's Personality Parade," *Parade*, April 5, 2009

The inquisitive, boundary-testing Little Billy was "born" out of a mix of boredom and a serendipitous surplus of postage stamps back in the carefree mid-1990s. Billy was conjured up by my thirty-year-old brain during the lengthy period of unemployment that naturally followed my whimsical move to Los Angeles to become a writer. When the magical Hollywood job failed to materialize, I had way too much time on my hands and I began searching for a creative outlet that did not involve my couch and the remote. One day on a rare expedition outside my apartment, I found a bundle of the aforementioned stamps in a vending machine at the local post office. It was about this very moment that I felt the first kicks of my demented inner child trying to get out. The first "Billy letters" went out shortly thereafter, and the initial responses from members of the Supreme Court and former Vice President Dan Quayle unleashed a giddy, stupid thrill that proved to be addictive. Indeed, the new correspondence hobby provided such low-cost, low-effort amusement that the charade went on . . . and on.

The ageless Little Billy has sought out the wise counsel of a wide range of personalities—from Mister Rogers to Mister Manson—on issues as disparate as McDonald's food and time travel. Like most passive-aggressive children, Billy likes to get multiple opinions on many of his inquiries. Who *wouldn't* want a sanity check on the Night Stalker's advice to stay in school?

*Nonagenarians say the
damndest things!*

To ___ Billy Geerhart ___

From *Art Linkletter*

January 6, 1999

Dear Billy:

In the whole history of the world there
is no worse time to quit school than now.

In the next 50 years of your life, people
who do not have an education will be
second class poor people.

We are now in the Age of Information and
Knowledge and Education. Think of the
Internet. Think of the Computer.

Finish school. High School and also
a college degree, or some special training for the computer world.

No young person today can afford to
quit school.

Good luck to you,

[signature]

AL:lr
P.S. Sorry, I no longer send out autographed photographs.

Now it is show-and-tell time because, as Billy might say, "What good are these letters if no one reads them?" Billy is a big proponent of sharing while his "father" has always been more of a brooding introvert. But you've probably skipped ahead, anyway. Regardless, we hope that the twisted correspondence herein offers you a unique and entertaining window into how the powerful, mundane, psychotic, and fictional (thanks NESQUIK Bunny!) deal with an impudent child—a child who, in the end, just wants attention (and the occasional high-end consumer product).

Art Linkletter

This legendary radio and television host, author, and commercial pitchman made his name interviewing children on the long-running programs *House Party* and *Kids Say the Darndest Things*. In honor of Mr. Linkletter's distinguished show business legacy of working with youngsters, Billy insisted that the book open with his letter.

Little Billy's Letters

Mr. Billy Geerhart

April 14, 1999

Dear Billy,

I was suprised to receiv...
being honest with ...
school ...
how c...
encou...
things...
Because...
I mean...

Als...
past is ...
were dest...
day.

I have...
I did and w...
anything if...
everything job...
But to my...
of teenagers,...
in other...

[Operation Drop Out]

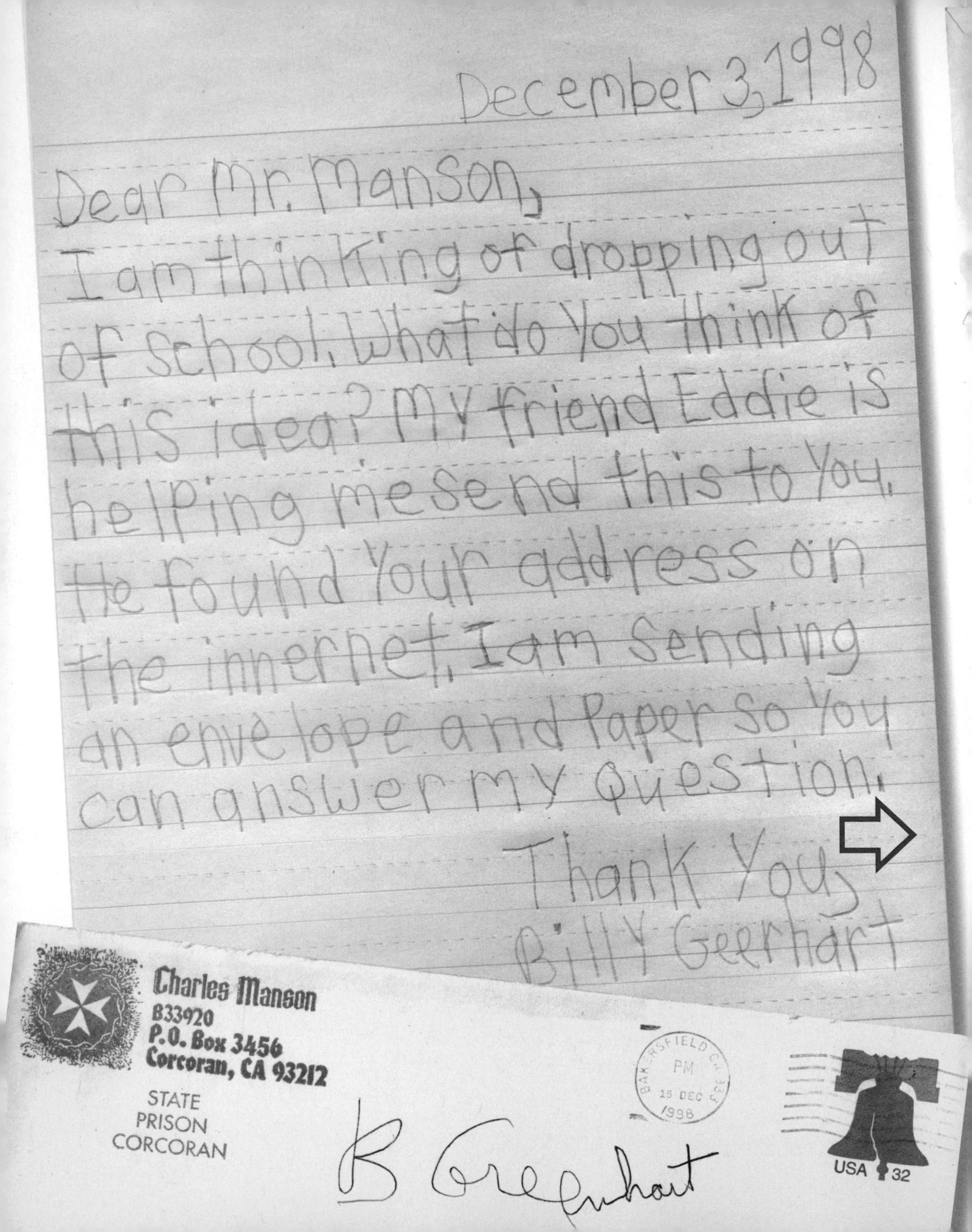

December 3, 1998

Dear Mr. Manson,
I am thinking of dropping out of school. What do you think of this idea? My friend Eddie is helping me send this to you. He found your address on the innernet. I am sending an envelope and paper so you can answer my question.

Thank You,
Billy Geerhart

Charles Manson
B33920
P.O. Box 3456
Corcoran, CA 93212

STATE
PRISON
CORCORAN

BAKERSFIELD CA 933
PM
15 DEC
1998

B Geerhart

USA 32

I RON HEAD
SPIDER BED
WWWEB

RECYCLED

*Find out why the L.A.
Times hasn't sent my
newspaper—
Charles Manson
P.S. O-yes Hi Billy
Easy easy eassy*

Find out why the L.A. Times hasn't sent my news paper— Charles Mac Manson P.S. O-yes Hi Billy Easy easy EASSY

Charles Manson

The former Scientologist, Beach Boys collaborator, and face of modern evil masterminded the Tate-LaBianca murders as leader of the Los Angeles–based cult known as The Family. Over the course of two consecutive nights in 1969, Charlie's crazed hippie minions took the lives of seven people including pregnant Hollywood starlet Sharon Tate, wife of film director Roman Polanski. The killings were intended to be the kickoff to a demented scheme known as "Helter Skelter" in which Manson would ultimately rule the world after a race war. The bearded, swastika-tattooed bogeyman now resides at Corcoran State Prison in California where every few years he reminds America of his psychosis in televised parole hearings.

I bet you don't remember
this—you dont even
know where its at
HAHA I got you
there
Charles Manson
Easy Billy

➡

Mr. Manson's barn photo didn't make much sense, but it
sure freaked out Little Billy's parents. It was around
this time Mr. Geerhart bought his first gun.

Tori Spelling

Tori is an actress and the daughter of legendary television producer Aaron Spelling. Her major claim to fame is playing a Catholic virgin for seven seasons on her father's hit show *Beverly Hills, 90210* (she was a discreet nonvirgin for the remaining three years of the series). Tori has also starred in the memorably titled TV movies *Mother, May I Sleep with Danger, Co-ed Call Girl,* and *Mind Over Murder.*

Best Wishes ♡ always, Tori Spelling "DONNA" '90210'

90210

LOS ANGELES
JUN 15 '99
CA
PB METER
6767507

U.S.POSTAGE
0.20

TAMKIN COLOR

Bill Gerhart

SPELLING
ENTERTAINMENT GROUP INC.

[FUN FACT]

In 2008 Spelling published the bestselling memoir *sTORI Telling* that features a description of an enraged Shannen Doherty smashing a $2,000 crystal dolphin.

> TED KACZYNSKI
> to
> BILLY GEERHART
>
> March 30, 1999
>
> Dear Mr. Geerhart:
>
> I can't advise you about whether to drop out of school, because I don't know anything about you. In order to give you advice of that kind I would have to know you very well and know a great deal about your situation.
>
> I'm sorry that I can't help you with advice, but, whatever you decide to do, I wish you the best of luck.
>
> Yours sincerely,
>
> Ted Kaczynski

Theodore Kaczynski, aka the Unabomber

Little Billy's brother informed him upon delivery of Mr. Kaczynski's missive that he was the first person in history to be excited to get a letter from the Unabomber.

This murderous neo-Luddite and Harvard man (class of '62) earned his nickname for a series of bombs he mailed to universities and airlines from 1978 to 1995. The former mathematician's explosive shipments killed three people and injured twenty-three. In 1995, he offered to desist from violence if the *Washington Post* or the *New York Times* would publish his antitechnology manifesto officially titled "Industrial Society and Its Future." The *Post* ran the entire 35,000-word screed, which led to Kaczynski's brother recognizing certain phrases and turning him in to the Feds. After pleading guilty in 1998 in a deal that spared him the death penalty, Kaczynski began serving his life sentence at Colorado's Supermax prison where he lives in a cell that has a bed, shower, sink, toilet, and—worst of all—a TV/radio. In 2008, the former mountain man objected to his less glamorous 10' × 12' foot cabin being put on display at the Newseum in Washington, D.C., as part of an exhibit on the FBI. His objections were disregarded.

Ian Ziering

This actor is best known for portraying the hairline-challenged high school/college student Steve Sanders on Fox's *Beverly Hills, 90210* from 1990 to 2000. In 2007, he finished eighth on ABC's *Dancing with the Stars*.

[FUN FACT]

Once married to *Playboy*'s Playmate of the Month for September 1997 (the former Nikki Schieler), he insists on the pretentious, actor-y pronunciation of his first name (*I*-en).

90210

ANGELES
CA
MAR-2'99

U.S. POSTAGE
0 2 0
PB METER
6767507

Billy Gearhart

TAMKIN COLOR

SPELLING ENTERTAINMENT GROUP INC.

Mr. Billy Geerhart

April 14, 1999

Dear Billy,

I was suprised to receive your letter. If you are being honest with me about thinking of dropping out of school, I would tell you not to do it. I do not know how old you are or what your situation is. But I would encourage you to hang in there and don't do self-destructive things. Don't throw your life away or waste it. Why? Because your life is precious to yourself and to God. I mean it.

Also, you seem to think that what happened in the past is some kind of joke. Let me tell you that lives were destroyed and people are hurting till this very day.

I have a lot of grief and guilt because of what I did and what I had become a part of. I would give anything if I could go back in time and have stopped everything before it started. I was the devil's fool. But today I have shared my story with tens of thousands of teenagers, prisoners, both in the United States and in other countries. I am no longer living in the past.

God bless you, Billy.

Yours truly,

David Berkowitz

David Berkowitz, aka Son of Sam

The Brooklyn-born Berkowitz was a mailman and former auxiliary policeman who terrorized New York City during a yearlong violence spree in 1976–1977 that left six people dead and seven others wounded. In psychotic letters to police and the media, he called himself "Son of Sam"—a reference to a demon he believed to be living in his neighbor's dog. Sentenced to 365 years in prison, Berkowitz later claimed that the killings were motivated not by a satanic Labrador retriever, but by the Hall & Oates song "Rich Girl."

Please do not dropout of School

Best of everything ♡ Claire Danes

Billy Geerhart

© NOT FOR REPRODUCTION

Claire Danes

In the mid-1990s Danes was the angst-ridden East Coast intellectual answer to the vacuous adolescent characters of *Beverly Hills, 90210*. Her series, *My So-Called Life*, lasted only one season, but she quickly graduated to a distinguished film career—an outcome that eluded her teen-show contemporaries.

Little Billy was happy that Claire (or her personal assistant) dashed off a quick scribble pleading with him to remain in school. It made all the difference in the world!

January 4, 1999

Dear Richard,

I am thinking of dropping out of school. What do you think of this idea? My friend Eddie said I should ask you.

Thank you,
Billy

P.S. I'm giving you some paper for your reply

Richard Ramirez, aka the Night Stalker

The pentagram-loving, AC/DC-adoring Ramirez was convicted in 1989 of thirteen killings and thirty other counts including attempted murder and multiple sexual assaults. Since his capture in 1985, the Night Stalker has developed a peculiar, mostly female fan base that has included Zeena LaVey Schreck, the daughter of Church of Satan founder Anton Szandor LaVey, and various murder groupies hoping to win the serial killer's black heart. In 1996, a forty-one-year-old self-proclaimed virgin by the name of Doreen Lioy bested her demented competition and wed Ramirez in a no-frills ceremony on San Quentin's Death Row where the groom still resides.

NightStalker

E37101 • SAN QUENTIN, CA 94964

Billy,
Greetings. Got yr letter. What school do you go to? Who's yr friend? You should stay in school. Send pictures.
Richard

Billy,
Greetings. Got yr letter. What school do you go to? Who's yr friend? You should stay in school. Send pictures.
Richard

Richard Ramirez E37101
San Quentin Prison 5E76
San Quentin CA
94964

SAN QUENTIN
STATE PRISON

SAN QUENTIN
JAN 21 '99
CALIF.

U.S. POSTAL
0.00
USA H
First-Class Rate

B. Geerhart

300271820

march 27, 1999

Dear Erik,

I wrote to you a long time ago about whether I should drop out of school. Maybe my letter got lost or something. I wanted to send you a stamp, but my friend Eddie said you couldn't send stuff like that. Anyway I would Really like to hear from you. Please write me back.

Thank you,
Billy Geerhart

Erik Menendez

Erik, along with his older brother Lyle (the bald one), infamously shotgunned their parents to death in their Beverly Hills mansion in 1989, but they were not considered suspects until months later. Before being arrested in 1990 the murderous siblings went on wild spending sprees that included a hot wings franchise for Lyle and tennis pro lessons for the more modest Erik. Guilt-ridden, Erik confessed the killings to his psychiatrist, which helped pave the way for the pair's arrest and sensational trials. The jury in the first trial deadlocked, but the brothers were convicted and sentenced to life without the possibility of parole in the second. Erik has been married for over ten years to Tammi Ruth Saccoman who published a memoir of their relationship entitled *They Said We'd Never Make It,* which the always reliable Larry King called "a heck of a book." The brothers, who reside in separate California prisons, have reportedly not spoken with one another in over a decade.

Dear Billy

I apologize for the length of time it has taken me to respond. That will not happen again. Tell me a little about yourself Billy. How old are you, why do you want to drop out of school? Are you having problems at school? What sort of things do you do with yourself self hobbies etc. It is hard for me to imagine that you should drop out of school. Fill me in some more on the details of your life.

I Am here and would like to listen to you and do what I can to help you billy, But I really need to know more about you. No need to send Stamps or that sort of thing. Thank you though Billy.

Your Friend
Erik

7-99

Little Billy was very impressed with Erik's penmanship! He hopes to be able to write in cursive script someday.

Dear Billy
I apologize for the length of time it has taken me to respond. That will not happen again. Tell me a little about yourself Billy. How old are you, why do you want to drop out of school? Are you having problems at school? What sort of things do you do with yourself hobbies etc. It is hard for me to imagine that you should drop out of school. Fill me in some more on the details of your life.

I am here and would like to listen to you and do what I can to help you billy, But I really need to know more about you. No need to send stamps or that sort of thing. Thank you though Billy.

Your Friend
Erik

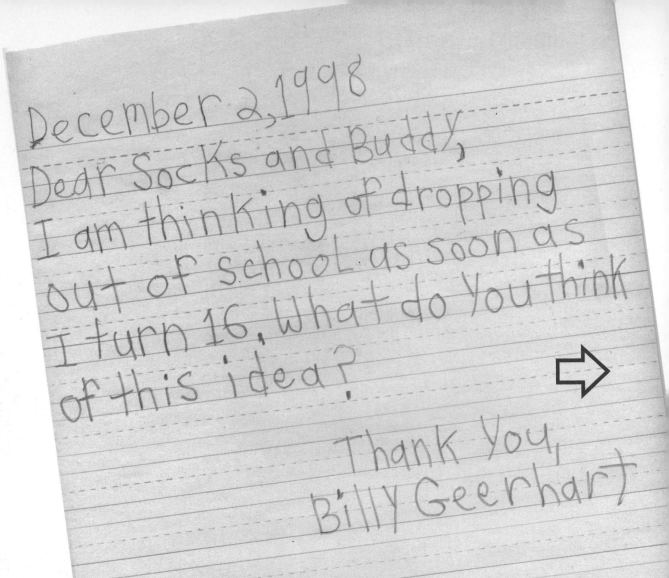

December 2, 1998

Dear Socks and Buddy,

I am thinking of dropping out of school as soon as I turn 16. What do you think of this idea?

Thank You,
Billy Geerhart

Socks and Buddy Clinton

Socks was a two-term First Cat brought to the White House when Bill Clinton won the presidency in 1992. Buddy, a chocolate Labrador retriever, was a second-term addition who arrived a year or so before his master's 1998 impeachment in the wake of the Monica Lewinsky scandal. Republican Congressman Dan Burton of Indiana, a fierce Clinton critic and Whitewater conspiracy theorist, once challenged the propriety of using White House personnel to answer fan mail addressed to Socks—an objection that was roundly ridiculed. Buddy was enjoying his apparently off-leash retirement years in Chappaqua, New York, when he was tragically hit by a car and killed. Socks, who was adopted by a Clinton aide, was put to sleep in 2009 after being diagnosed with cancer of the jaw. Like Nixon's cocker spaniel Checkers and FDR's Scottish terrier, Fala, both Socks and Buddy received *New York Times* death coverage.

Thank you for writing to me. I am honored to be your "First Cat."

So...

THE WHITE HOUSE

Thank you for writing to me. Living at the White House is very exciting, and I am enjoying my new family.

Buddy

PRINTED ON RECYCLED PAPER

Jesus Is Lord, Over All!
Charles D. Watson B-37999
P.O. Box 409000 B6-218L
Ione, CA 95640

Dear Billy:

4/18/99

Thanks for your letter. Eddie is right, you should not quit school. The more school you have, the better job you will be able to get.

I have two teenage boys who have learned that they have to work very hard to make only $6 an hour. So they are getting all the school available so they can make $50 an hour and not have to work as hard. They are learning all they can about computers.

It is very important to hang around friends who are going in a positive direction. School is a positive direction. Church is a positive direction. Family is a positive direction. Obeying your mom and dad is a positive direction. Listening to older children who are going in a positive direction is a positive direction.

I am enclosing a brochure that may help you to see how I went in the wrong direction, how I was deceived by the negative world, but how God came into my life and go me going in the right direction. Since that time my life has been blessed. See, the negative direction brings a curse, but the positive direction brings blessings. As a Christian, this is walking in faith.

If you have a computer at school or home, check out our ministry website on the internet. I will have you in my prayers for wisdom to do the right thing. And stay in school, this is most important.

Your friend in Christ,

Charles

Billy Geerhart

Charles "Tex" Watson

This former high school football star and chief lieutenant to Charles Manson took the lead in the 1969 Tate-LaBianca murders and was convicted in all seven killings. After renouncing Manson and becoming a born-again Christian, he managed to sire four children from behind bars with wife/groupie Kristen Joan Svega. It took a 1996 California state ruling banning conjugal visits for life sentence inmates to finally stop Watson from procreating (he and the Mrs. stuck it out until 2003 before divorcing). These days Charlie's former enforcer spends most of his time running his Abounding Love Ministries from his cell at Mule Creek State Prison.

[FUN FACT]

In his 1978 autobiography, *Will You Die for Me?* Watson takes credit for introducing an unsuspecting Dennis Wilson to Manson after picking the Beach Boy up hitchhiking.

Thanks for the note, here
is the photo you wanted.
I hope you like it!

You Rock!
Rosie

Rosie O'Donnell

The 1984 *Star Search* winner, TV talk-show host, actress, author, and gay-rights advocate served
a short, turbulent stint on ABC's *The View* in 2007 during which she repeatedly reduced her
conservative co-panelist Elisabeth Hasselbeck to tears.

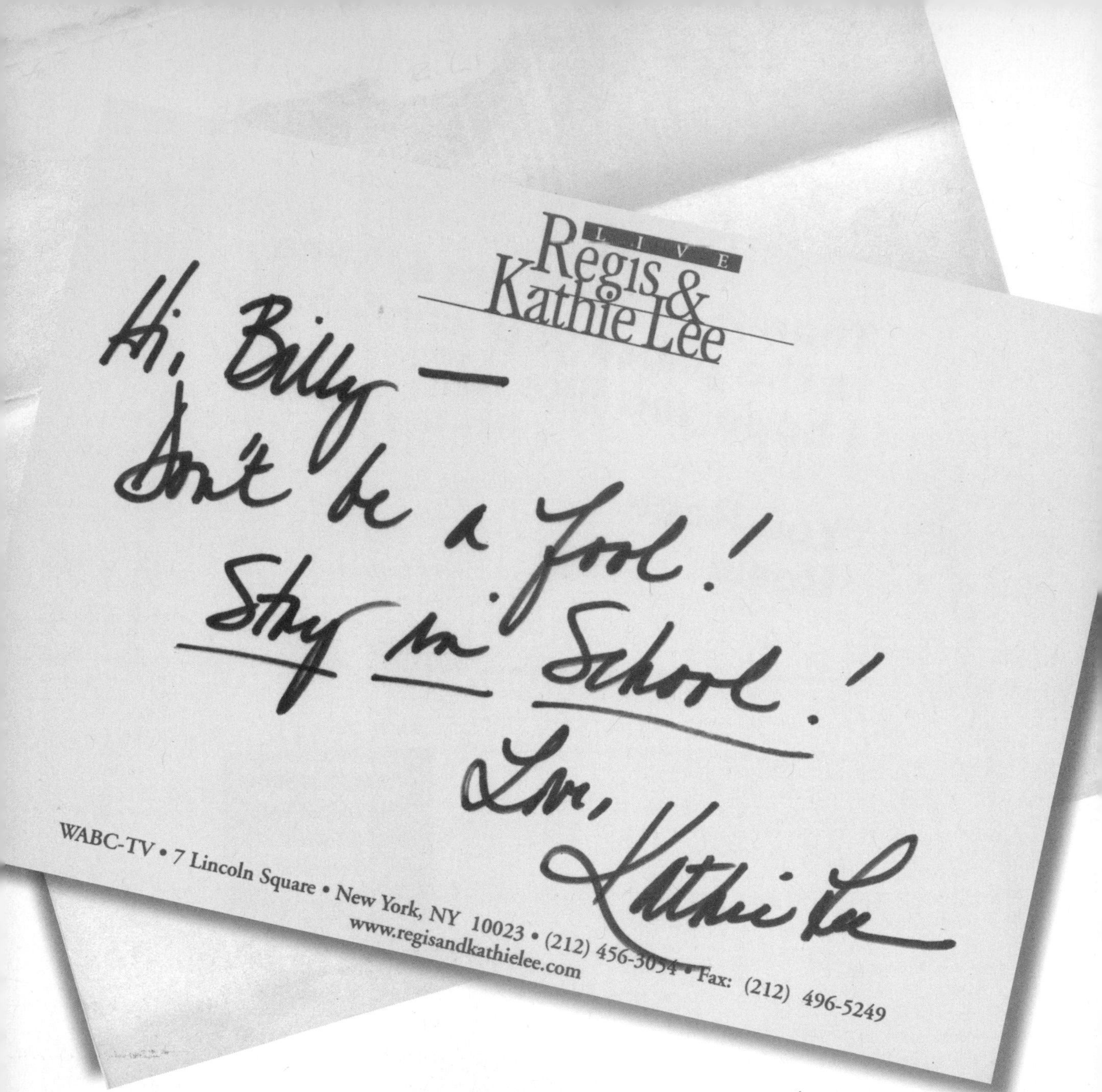

LIVE
**Regis &
Kathie Lee**

Hi, Billy —
Don't be a fool!
Stay in School!
Love,
Kathie Lee

WABC-TV • 7 Lincoln Square • New York, NY 10023 • (212) 456-3054 • Fax: (212) 496-5249
www.regisandkathielee.com

Kathy Lee Gifford

The 1971 Junior Miss beauty queen from Maryland, born-again
Christian, wife of retired leatherhead Frank Gifford, and former TV
foil to Regis Philbin now cohosts what feels like the tenth hour of
The Today Show on NBC.

*Kathy Lee's advice
sounds an awful lot
like Mr. T's.*

The Dr. Laura Program

Dr. Laura sure made a lot of sense to Little Billy. And unlike the commitment-phobic Unabomber, she at least gave him something to think about.

April 10 '99

Dear Billy—

Whenever you think about making a serious decision—stop and imagine yourself twenty years in the future looking back at this moment. Would you feel proud seeing yourself give up on school? If you need help—get it. But never give up on yourself.

warmly—L Schlessinger

15260 Ventura Boulevard • Suite 500 • Sherman Oaks • California 91403-5339 • (818) 461-5403 • Fax (818) 461-5440
Web Site: www.drlaura.com

April 10 '99
Dear Billy—
Whenever you think about making a serious
decision—stop and imagine yourself twenty
years in the future looking back at this
moment. Would feel proud seeing yourself
give up on school? If you need help—get it.
But never give up on yourself.
Warmly,
L. Schlessinger

Dr. Laura Schlessinger

This radio talk-show host/self-help guru practices a particularly entertaining form of tough love that appeals to sadists (the audience) and masochists (the callers). Schlessinger, who is also a best-selling author, has a Ph.D. in physiology from Columbia University, and a certification in Marriage, Family and Child Counseling from the University of Southern California.

March 30, 1999

Dear Billy,

I don't know who your friend Eddie is, but I'm glad that he suggested that you ask me what I think. I'm not so sure how 'cool' someone can be after spending 30 years of her life in prison, but I certainly appreciate Eddie's confidence in me.

I was 17, nearly 18 when I quite high school Billy. It was a big mistake. It was the first in a very long line of bad mistakes. Each bad choice I made after quitting school cost me more and more and more. Not in money or anything like that. But in dignity, self-respect, and the consequences of each wrong choice got worse and worse. How smart was I? I'm in prison, Billy. That isn't what I call being very smart or very cool.

Now, some 32 years after I quit school, I'm alot older and wiser, hopefully a wee bit cool, and very well educated. I went back to school, Billy. I got my G.E.D., from inside a prison cell, and while I've been here in this prison, I went on to college, I've got an Associate of Arts Degree, I'm presently at nearly 51 years of age, working on my Bachelor of Arts Degree. I've completed several Vocational Training Programs, including Data Processing, Word Processing, and I'm a certified Para-Legal.

I'll tell you honestly, Billy, I didn't like high school. That's only because I didn't think I was smart. I wasn't popular, and that world out there looked so big and so inviting. But I wasn't prepared for it. I thought I was being cool when I quit. I fell flat on my face and landed myself in prison.

It is not always easy, Billy, to do the right thing. Sometimes doing the right thing, the smart thing, like staying in school and toughing it out takes a great deal more courage than turning and quiting.

I think you are pretty smart, Billy. You listened to your firend, Eddie, you took the time to write to a complete stranger and ask someone older, "what do you think? That took courage, you risked something, Billy. I pray, with all my heart that you have the courage to listen to me, stick it out, hang in there. Get your high school diploma. I don't know what grade you are in, or how old you are, but someday, you'll really be glad that you didn't quit school.

I will be praying for you, Billy, and asking God to help you to make the right choice, not the easy choice, but the right one. The measure of a man is often times found not in his height or weight, or how much money he has, or what job he has, or even how many people think he's really cool, but the measure of a man is found in the quality of his character. Character is defined as moral excellence and firmness. If you don't know what that means yet, you might want to stay in school long enough to find out, so that you may become a man of moral excellence and firmness. Now that's what I call cool!

A person with an education has more opportunity to see what alternatives there are available to them. Be a young man of courage and strength, and

you will be come a man whose virtue is built on seeing that anything worth
having, an education is worth having, is worth working for. Although you
live in America and have been given as a birth right, freedom of choice, you
can choose what to do with the rest of your life, Billy, that freedom comes
with the awesome responsiblity, that every choice you make, every day, has
consequences.

Make smart choices, Billy. Build a life, one day at a time....sometimes
that means one homework assignment at a time, one test at a time, enduring
one more gruelling class room or unreasonable teacher, or horrible day in
a place you just cant stand. Endurance will build character. Real character
is cool.

May you make the right choice, Billy. You now have the benefit of knowing
what I think about quitting school. It isn't in your BEST interest.

Very truly yours,

Mrs. Susan Atkins-Whitehouse

PS

Billy, I'm married to a man of character, who cooler than cool, seriously.
He's a college graduate, a Harvard Law School graduate, and a private attorney
today. It wasn't easy for him to make the right choices...but he did. He's
a very smart man. You also can be a very smart young man.
You will be in my prayers.

Susan Atkins-Whitehouse, aka Sexy Sadie, aka Sadie Mae Glutz

The infamous Manson "girl" was convicted of all seven of the 1969 Tate-LaBianca murders as
well as the killing of Family acquaintance Gary Hinman. Atkins initially bragged of stabbing
pregnant Hollywood starlet Sharon Tate to death, but later claimed that she had never killed
anyone. Charles "Tex" Watson takes sole responsibility for the murder of Tate in his 1978
book, *Will You Die for Me?* Before falling under Charlie's spell, Atkins was a topless dancer
in San Francisco. She also briefly worked for Church of Satan founder Anton Szandor LaVey
in a stage production in which she played a disrobing vampire. Incredibly, the notorious
murderess has been married twice in prison, most recently to her lawyer, a Harvard man.

April 1, 1999

Dear Mrs. Whitehouse,

You must have a lot of spare time! That was the longest letter I've ever gotten! My friend Eddie said you were cool because he saw you on T.V. with Charles Manson and Squeeky (?). He said you guys did some cool stuff in the '60's. Did you know the Beetles? I wrote to all these people because I want to make a good decision.

②

Mr. Manson sent me a strange picture of a shack or house in the grass. Do you know what that means!?! He did not really answer my question. He drew on the paper, to. Anyway, you seem very nice and I have decided to stay in school. I cant quit until I'm 16 anyway. Your husband must be great. Is he trying to get you out of jail? Can I send you stamps?

Best wishes,
Billy

April 6, 1999

Dear Billy,

Thank you for your letter of April 1, 1999. I'm really glad to hear that you are going to stay in school. At least I now know about how old you are. You aren't 16 yet, so that means you are somewhere between 6 and 15! Smile. So, how old are you?

I don't think I'm cool, Billy! Certainly not because of anything having to do with Charles Manson. He is not cool, either. Anytime anyone decides to order young kids to kill innocent people, they loose cool status! Lots and lots and lots of people suffered horribly because of Charles Manson. I certainly wish that I'd never met him.

I don't think it's a good idea to write Charles Manson, Billy. He is not a nice man. I don't care what anyone else says, I knew him. I'm in prison because of things he made me do, and there are 9 people who are dead because of him.

I also don't know what the pictures mean that he sent you. I do not communicate with him at all, and have not communicated with him for nearly 28 years.

Thanks for offering to send me stamps, Billy. I have enough, thank you. When it is time for me to come out of prison, God will make a way. Until then, my husband and I are very happy together, and he really is a nice man.

I honestly don't have a lot of spare time, Billy. I work 8 hours a day, 5 days a week at my State assigned prison job. I'm currently enrolled in a correspondence college program, I do Bible Studies, visit with my husband 3 times a week, and am always doing something. But your letter was so sweet, and your question so sincere, I decided to write to you.

When I was a young girl, I would probably not have gotten into to the trouble I had gotten into if someone older had taken an interest in me and tried to help me believe in myself. That's why I'm writing to you. I think you are a nice young man, with a lot of potential, and I pray that you will work real hard and become the very best you that you can become. Staying in school will give you the education to do just that. Life is so precious, Billy. It has so many wonderful things to show us. AND, inside of you there are so many wonderful things that you can contribute to life to make this a better world.

Sincerely,

Susan

Little Billy's prison pen pal died of brain cancer in 2009.

We
my
har
co
or
ple

is a project for school.
are doing a unit on just
eacher says you
s people

[Billy's Law]

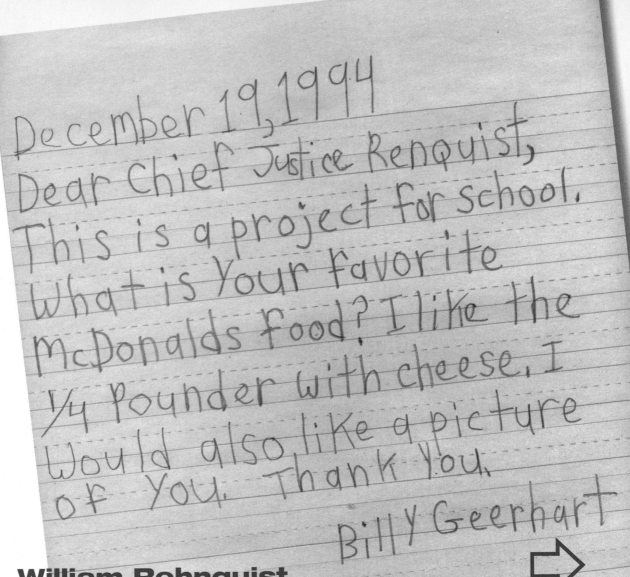

December 19, 1994

Dear Chief Justice Renquist,

This is a project for school.
What is your favorite
McDonalds food? I like the
1/4 pounder with cheese. I
would also like a picture
of you. Thank you.

Billy Geerhart

William Rehnquist

This stylish jurist was appointed to the Supreme Court by President Richard Nixon in 1971 and elevated to Chief Justice in 1983 by President Ronald Reagan. Rehnquist, an author of four books on legal history, chose to make a little history of his own when he added four yellow stripes to his judicial robe in 1995. He decided on this unusual fashion statement after admiring similar "flair" on the Lord Chancellor character's costume in a stage production of Gilbert and Sullivan's comic opera *Iolanthe*. The bestriped Chief Justice presided over the senate impeachment trial and acquittal of Bill Clinton in 1999 and then helped elect George W. Bush president with the controversial *Bush v. Gore* ruling in 2000. Rehnquist passed away in 2005 at the age of eighty, and his more modestly robed replacement, John Roberts, has, thus far, reserved his judicial creativity for winging the presidential oath of office.

Supreme Court of the United States
Washington, D. C. 20543

February 8, 1995

Mr. Billy Geerhart

Dear Mr. Geerhardt:

On behalf of Chief Justice Rehnquist, I am responding to
your letter requesting information on the Chief Justice.
Although he is unable to personally respond to your letter, I
have enclosed a booklet about the Supreme Court and a photograph
of the Chief Justice.

Sincerely,

Harvey Rishikof

Enclosures
HR:smg

WILLIAM REHNQUIST 27

Supreme Court of the United States
Washington, D. C. 20543

CHAMBERS OF
JUSTICE CLARENCE THOMAS

January 10, 1995

Billy Geerhart

Dear Billy:

Thank you for your recent letter. I sincerely appreciate your taking the time to write to me. As you have requested, I am enclosing a copy of my official photograph.

Best wishes for a successful school year.

Sincerely,

Clarence Thomas

Clarence Thomas

I like the Egg McMuffin. Actually, I like almost everything there.

Enclosure

Clarence Thomas

Justice Thomas is, by most accounts, the Supreme Court's most reliable pornography expert since Potter Stewart retired from the bench in 1981. His dramatic senate confirmation hearings, in which he was accused of sexual harassment by Anita Hill, were notable for bringing together the words "pubic hair" and "Coke can" for the first time in the history of the *Congressional Record*. When not sitting silently during oral arguments or rubber-stamping Antonin Scalia's legal opinions, the fun-loving jurist likes to smoke cigars and travel the country in a giant RV.

CHAMBERS OF
JUSTICE SANDRA DAY O'CONNOR

December 30, 1994

Billy Greenhart

Dear Billy:

Justice O'Connor thanks you for your letter. Her favorite food at McDonalds is a Big Mac. She asked me to send the enclosed picture.

Sincerely,

Carolyn H. Sand
Administrative Secretary

Sandra Day O'Connor

Sandra Day O'Connor

This former elected judge and state senator from Arizona was appointed by President Ronald Reagan in 1981 to be the first woman to serve on the Supreme Court. As a justice, she angered conservatives by providing the swing vote in upholding *Roe v. Wade* in the case of *Planned Parenthood v. Casey* in 1992. In 2000, she made conservatives happy by joining the majority in *Bush v. Gore*. O'Connor retired from the court in 2006.

CHAMBERS OF
JUSTICE RUTH BADER GINSBURG

December 28, 1994

Billy Geerhart

Dear Billy:

The Justice asked me to tell you she loves Chinese, Italian, and French cooking, but hasn't been to McDonald's since her son was 10. (He is now 29.)

Sincerely,

Linda C. O'Donnell

Linda C. O'Donnell
Secretary to
Justice Ginsburg

Ruth Bader Ginsburg

Ruth Bader Ginsburg

The former law school professor and appeals court judge for the D.C. circuit was appointed in 1993 as the second woman to the Supreme Court by President Bill Clinton. Ginsburg generally votes with the liberal wing of the court, but likes to hang out socially with conservative justice Antonin Scalia—they go to the opera together.

Supreme Court of the United States
Washington, D.C. 20543

CHAMBERS OF
JUSTICE DAVID H. SOUTER

January 23, 1995

Dear Billy:

I enclose a picture, but I'm afraid I can't tell you very much about McDonald's food.

Yours sincerely,

David Souter

Master Billy Geerhart

David Souter

The New England native and appeals judge was appointed to the Supreme Court by President George H. W. Bush in 1990 and was dubbed the "stealth nominee" by the press because of his lack of a judicial paper trail. Souter, who was unfairly opposed by Democrats at the time of his confirmation hearings, later infuriated conservatives when he aligned himself with the liberal wing of the court. When the next vacancy opened up a year later, Bush took no chances and appointed the certifiably right-wing Clarence Thomas. Souter retired from the bench in 2009.

January 5, 1995

CHAMBERS OF
JUSTICE HARRY A. BLACKMUN
RETIRED

Mr. Billy Geerhart

Dear Billy:

I have been out of the city for a few days and am delayed in answering your letter of December 19. You ask me about my favorite McDonald's food. Almost anything they put out is acceptable. I like to go to Roy Rogers, too, for a beef sandwich. But I hope most of all that you eat something more than what these fast food places put out. A hamburger and fries or potato chips are all right in their place, but you need some fruits and vegetables, too. I suspect your mom would tell you so.

Sincerely,

Harry A. Blackmun

Harry Blackmun

President Richard Nixon appointed this lifelong Republican to the Supreme Court in 1970 with the aim of making the institution more conservative. But within three years of being seated on the bench, the justice had authored the *Roe v. Wade* opinion igniting a seemingly endless culture war on legalized abortion. By the time Blackmun stepped down in 1994, he was the court's most liberal member and a passionate pro-choice advocate. Hopefully the esteemed jurist managed to enjoy a few Happy Meals during his retirement years before passing away in 1999 at the age of ninety.

Supreme Court of the United States
Washington, D. C. 20543

January 25, 1995

In keeping with the verbosity of
his legal opinions, Justice Scalia's
nonresponse is longer than most of
his colleagues' fast-food rulings.

Mr. William D. Geerhart

Dear Mr. Geerhart:

Justice Scalia does not have time to respond to information requests.
He regrets that fact, but hopes you will understand the demands on his time,
and the number of such requests he receives, do not permit it.

Sincerely,

Mary Ellen Donshill
Secretary to Justice Scalia

Antonin Scalia

The Supreme Court's most outspoken and combative conservative was appointed in 1986 by
President Ronald Reagan. Scalia, whose nomination was supported by liberals such as New York
governor Mario Cuomo, was the first Italian American on the court.

December 8, 1998

Dear Ms. Reno,
This is a project for my school.
We are supposed to write to
someone we admire and ask a
question. I want to know
who you think is a better crime
fighter — Batman or the
Terminator? My Dad is helping
me send this. Please send me
a signed picture!

Thank you,
Billy Geerhart

Janet Reno

This tough, tall Danish American was elected to four terms as state attorney for Dade County in Florida before becoming the first female U.S. attorney general in history under President Bill Clinton. During her controversial eight-year tenure she crushed the Branch Davidian cult standoff in Waco, Texas; helped make Richard Jewell's life miserable (before apologizing); and sent little Elian Gonzalez back to Cuba after the boy's heavily armed "rescue" from a relative's home in Miami.

Office of the Attorney General
Washington, D.C.

March 1, 1999

Mr. Billy Geerhart

Dear Billy:

Thank you for your recent letter. I always enjoy hearing from students.

I read Batman comics when I was your age so I know of his efforts to fight crime better than I know the Terminator's work. We can all fight crime by trying the best we can to do the right thing and be the best person we can. Stand tall, be kind to others, and seek justice for all.

Sincerely,

Janet Reno

Janet Reno

To Billy Geerhart
Justice for all.
Janet Reno

[FUN FACT]

In more recent years, Reno ran for and lost the 2002 Florida governor's race and made a cameo appearance on the recurring *Saturday Night Live* sketch "Janet Reno's Dance Party" that featured Will Ferrell as the former attorney general.

July 4, 2001

Dear Mr. Shapiro,
My sister Connie told my parents that I killed her doll and I got punished even tho it was the dog that did it. No one believes me except my brother. He said you were real smart about law. Can I do anything to get my sister back or get people to believe me. Please write me back quick!   Thanks!
                                              Billy

Robert Shapiro

The quintessential Los Angeles power lawyer is best known for being the architect of O. J. Simpson's "Dream Team" of attorneys that won the former pro football star's acquittal on double murder charges in 1995. In 2009, with the Juice safely behind bars again after his Las Vegas burglary and kidnapping conviction, Shapiro told Fox News Online that he thought his former client was a "sociopath." Shapiro has also represented Johnny Carson, Christian Brando, and Linda Lovelace, among many others.

LAW OFFICES

CHRISTENSEN, MILLER, FINK, JACOBS, GLASER, WEIL & SHAPIRO, LLP

2121 AVENUE OF THE STARS
EIGHTEENTH FLOOR
LOS ANGELES, CALIFORNIA 90067-5010
(310) 553-3000
FAX (310) 556-2920

DIRECT DIAL NUMBER
(310) 556-7886
EMAIL: RSHAPIRO@CHRISMILL.COM

August 1, 2001

If Little Billy ever gets into trouble as an adult, Mr. Shapiro will be his first telephone call.

Billy Geerhart

Dear Billy:

Thank you for your letter dated July 4, 2001 regarding your recent conviction in the case of the murder of your sister's doll. You maintain that the crime was committed by the family dog and have asked me what you can do to convince your parents and your sister Connie that you are not guilty.

Unfortunately, you have already been punished for the deed, and the dog is not likely to voluntarily confess. Therefore, there are only a couple of ways in which you could prove your innocence. For instance, is there any forensic evidence that will support your theory that the dog killed the doll? Were any scraps of doll clothing found near his dog house, perhaps? How about tooth marks on the doll's remains (assuming there were remains)? If so, a good forensic dentist should be able to match them to the dog. In addition, a DNA expert may be able to determine that saliva found on the doll's body came from the dog. Finally, you might be able to find an alibi witness for the time of the doll's death (if, in fact, you know the time). That person could sign an affidavit saying that you could not possibly have committed the crime because you were with him (or her) at the time the murder took place.

I realize that this case is now closed and that any evidence that may have existed has likely been destroyed, and the doll has probably been given a decent burial. If indeed that is the case, then your problem lies in seeking redemption for an act you didn't commit. This will not be easy, since you are likely to have some feelings of bitterness. My best advice to you is that you not allow your indignation to get in the way of your desire to regain the respect of your parents and sister. You must be unfailingly respectful of their belongings and give them no reason to look to you when another doll turns up missing or dead.

Good luck, Billy, and please give my best regards to your brother.

Sincerely,

ROBERT L. SHAPIRO
of CHRISTENSEN, MILLER, FINK, JACOBS,
GLASER, WEIL & SHAPIRO, LLP

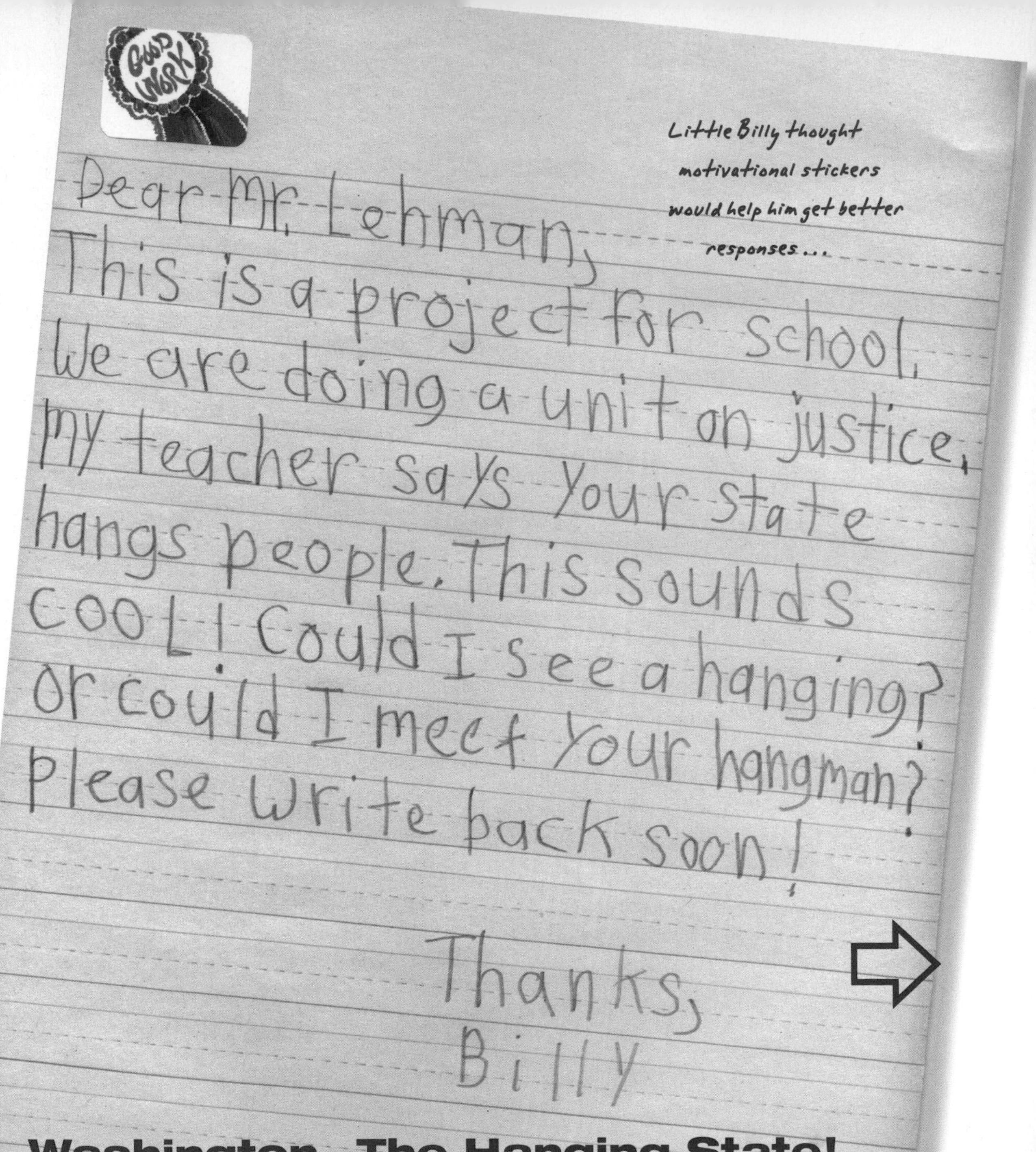

Dear Mr. Lehman,

This is a project for school. We are doing a unit on justice. My teacher says your state hangs people. This sounds COOL! Could I see a hanging? Or could I meet your hangman? Please write back soon!

Thanks,
Billy

Washington—The Hanging State!

Hanging is still an option for the condemned in Washington, but the default method of carrying out a death sentence is lethal injection. The most recent person to go to the gallows in the state was Charles Rodman Campbell in 1994. Campbell had been convicted in the 1982 knifing deaths of two women and a young girl.

STATE OF WASHINGTON

DEPARTMENT OF CORRECTIONS
OFFICE OF THE SECRETARY

P.O. Box 41101 • Olympia, Washington 98504-1101 • (360) 753-2500
FAX (360) 664-4056

January 28, 2002

Mr. Billy Geerhart

Dear Billy:

Thank you for your recent letter and for allowing me the opportunity to be involved in your class project. It was a pleasant surprise to receive correspondence from a young person who is interested in learning more about the criminal justice process.

A number of years ago the people of the state of Washington wanted to send a message that certain behaviors committed in the state were unacceptable and that the punishment should fit the crime. They decided that a suitable punishment for taking the life of another person is death. For a long time, the acceptable method to perform the punishment was hanging. Recently our state legislature changed the method of execution to lethal injection.

As head of the Department of Corrections, I have the ultimate responsibility to carry out an execution. This is a very serious responsibility and the hardest part of my job. From talking with staff throughout the department, but especially those at the facility where an execution must be carried out, the process is very difficult. It is not an easy task to put a human being to death; it is not something we do easily nor take lightly.

In both my professional and personal life, I work hard to assist people in getting the education, job training and treatment they need to better prepare them to fulfill their obligations in society. It is only by addressing these important issues that we can expect to break the cycle of recidivism, reduce the number of young people entering the system and finally eliminate crimes that result in a death sentence of an innocent person.

I compliment you on the work you completed on the school assignment and appreciate the opportunity to respond to your letter. Each of us has the responsibility to make a positive difference in the lives of others in our communities. I encourage you to work with your parents, teachers, and classmates, to find and value the best in others and to make a difference in your community.

Sincerely,

Joseph D. Lehman
Secretary

...Little Billy was wrong about the
motivational stickers helping him to get
better responses.

Dear Mr. Stanley,
This is a project for school.
We are doing a unit on Justice.
My teacher says your state
hangs people. This sounds
cool! could I see a hanging?
or could I meet your hangman?
please write back soon!

Thanks,
BILLY

New Hampshire—
the Other Hanging State!

If for some reason lethal injection cannot be administered, New Hampshire law specifies
hanging as the alternate method for carrying out the state's extremely rare death sentences.
The last person to be hanged in the state was Howard Long in 1939. Long had been convicted
of molesting and then bludgeoning a ten-year-old boy to death with a tire jack. Mr. Stanley no
doubt left this grisly detail out of his letter so as not to alarm Billy and his parents.

STATE OF NEW HAMPSHIRE
DEPARTMENT OF CORRECTIONS
OFFICE OF THE COMMISSIONER
PO BOX 1806
CONCORD, NH 03302-1806

603-271-5600   FAX: 603-271-5643
TDD Access: 1-800-735-2964

Phil Stanley
Commissioner

February 7, 2002

Mr. Billy Geerhart

Dear Mr. Geerhart:

Thank you for your letter about the State of New Hampshire's capital punishment law. New Hampshire has not put anyone to death for a crime since 1939. Your teacher is correct. Capital Punishment is still a sentence that a Judge may impose in New Hampshire.

Good luck with your justice project.

Sincerely,

Phil Stanley
Commissioner

Billy Geerhart

Dear Billy:

Thank you for your letter of November 29, reg...
president. I was involved in student po...
Student Council in junior high...

I think a good...
a voice!!...

I...

RR/lbi

47877   ATLANTA, GEOR...

[Class President]

December 10, 1994

Dear Mr. Quayle,
I wanted to write and tell
you my mother read me your
book and I liked it so much
I want to be Vice President
of my class, Would you support
Me? I would also like your
Picture!

Thanks,
Billy Geerhart

Dan Quayle

The youthful senator's image as a privileged, dunderheaded lightweight was crystallized during his first vice-presidential debate when Lloyd Bentsen famously dismissed him as being "no Jack Kennedy." Quayle's frequent missteps and gaffes while in office reached critical mass in 1992 when at a photo op in a public school classroom he instructed a twelve-year-old boy to add an "e" to his chalkboard spelling of the word "potato." Four years earlier, during his slogan-mangling speech to the United Negro College Fund, Quayle provided what would become the representative quote of his vice presidency: "What a waste it is to lose one's mind, or not to have a mind is being very wasteful. How true that is."

February 9, 1995

Dan Quayle sent Little Billy's family Christmas cards for two years before realizing that he wasn't donating to his exploratory presidential committee.

Mr. Billy Geerhart

Dear Billy:

Thank you for your recent letter. I am pleased that my book, *Standing Firm*, served as an inspiration for you to run as class vice president.

Enclosed with this letter is the signed photograph you requested.

Again, thank you for writing. Best wishes for success in this election and in all your future endeavors.

Sincerely,

Dan Quayle

DQ:js

Enclosure

To Billy—
Good luck—

November 9, 1998

Dear Mr. Starr,

This is a project for my school. We are supposed to write to a public official we admire and ask a question. My Dad is helping me send this. I am running for my class presidency. Could you wish me luck and send a photo? Thank you very much. I don't care what my friends say. I think your cool and when I grow up I want to be a lawyer.

Sincerely,
Billy

Kenneth Starr

As Independent Counsel, Starr investigated and obsessively documented President Bill Clinton's extramarital affair with White House intern Monica Lewinsky. The culmination of the twerpy former judge's seemingly endless persecution of Clinton was a salacious, taxpayer-funded porno novel entitled *The Starr Report*. Clinton was impeached over the findings, but went on to be acquitted in the Senate and complete his second term with the highest approval ratings of any postwar president. Starr is now the dean of the mediocre Pepperdine University Law School and counsel for conservative groups hoping to uphold the ban on same-sex marriage in California.

Office of the Independent Counsel

1001 Pennsylvania Avenue, N.W.
Suite 490-North
Washington, D.C. 20004
(202) 514-8688
Fax (202) 514-8802

November 23, 1998

Billy Geerhart

Dear Billy:

Thank you very much for your kind letter. Enclosed is an autographed photo for you. Good luck in the election for third grade class president. I'm sure your parents are extremely proud of you.

Best wishes for a great year!

Sincerely,

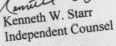

Kenneth W. Starr
Independent Counsel

Before Mr. Cheney became copresident, he had a lot more time on his hands....

Dick Cheney

This taciturn, occasionally profane ("F*** yourself!") torture enthusiast served as secretary of defense during Desert Storm, and then as CEO of Halliburton in the 1990s before becoming the forty-sixth vice president of the United States under George W. Bush. Cheney is best known for secretive multitasking, engineering the Iraq War, and shooting hunting buddy Harry Whittington in the face with a shotgun. The former vice president emerged from his undisclosed location in 2009 to begin a protracted self-serving critique of President Obama.

DICK CHENEY   11/20/98

To Billy Geerhart – I'm glad you
are interested in Desert Storm. And
good luck in your campaign to
be class president!

Dick Cheney

The overachieving Cheney received
five draft deferments, two DUIs, and
had four heart attacks all before
taking the oath as veep!

November 9, 1998

Dear Mrs. Reagan,

This is a project for my school. I am running for my class Presidency. I know President Reagan is not feeling very well. It would mean allot to me if you could send me a picture wishing me luck.

Thank you,

Billy Geerhart

Nancy Reagan

The former first lady began her career as an actress under her maiden name Nancy Davis and later made a mark in such B movies as *Donovan's Brain* and *Hellcats of the Navy*. Ms. Davis first met Ronald Reagan when he was head of the Screen Actors Guild and she needed help getting her name removed from the Hollywood blacklist (apparently there was some *other* Nancy Davis who was a Communist). It was a match made in Red Scare heaven—the couple married in 1952 and remained almost inseparable through their White House years and beyond.

OFFICE OF NANCY REAGAN

November 19, 1998

Dear Billy:

On behalf of Mrs. Reagan, thank you very much for your recent letter to her. Enclosed you will find a picture for you. Mrs. Reagan also asked me to write and wish you good luck in running for class president. It's great that you are participating in government! Keep up the good work.

Mrs. Reagan sends you and your classmates her warmest best wishes-- and remember, Billy, the old saying, "It's not whether you win or lose but how you play the game".

Sincerely,

Libbie Brady

Libbie Brady
Assistant to Mrs. Reagan

Mr. Billy Geerhart

To Billy Geerhart
Best Wishes
Nancy Reagan

[FUN FACT]

During her Just Say No drug awareness campaign in the 1980s, the first lady played herself in a "very special episode" of the sitcom *Diff'rent Strokes*. Her costars included future drug casualty Dana Plato and future recovering addict Todd Bridges.

To Billy Geerhart, congratulations on your candidacy for 3rd Grade President. Good luck.
Gerald R. Ford

Gerald Ford

This accident-prone president succeeded and then pardoned the disgraced Richard Nixon ending the "long national nightmare" of Watergate. Ford's image as a clumsy chief executive began when he fell down the steps of Air Force One in 1975, and it was solidified when Chevy Chase began satirizing him as a stumbling buffoon on *Saturday Night Live*. The same year the president survived two inept assassination attempts by psychotic women, one of whom was a disciple of Charles Manson. In 1976 Ford narrowly lost the presidential election to Jimmy Carter, which initiated his long retirement. After his death in 2006, interviews that the former president had given under embargo were published. Ford's beyond-the-grave commentary revealed that he thought Bill Clinton was a sex addict, Dick Cheney was a liability to the Republican Party, and the Iraq War was unjustified.

Mr. Dole is a member of the Greatest Generation, but my dad says he still got his ass kicked by a hippie in '96 (whatever that means).

To Billy,
Good Luck!!!

Bob Dole

This cranky World War II hero became a Republican senator from Kansas and President Gerald Ford's hatchet-man running mate in 1976 before running for the presidency himself twenty years later. Dole lost the election to incumbent Bill Clinton, but rebounded as a commercial pitchman for Viagra and Pepsi, appearing in a spot for the latter with Britney Spears. Dole was memorably portrayed by Norm McDonald on *Saturday Night Live* as an angry old man who always refers to himself in the third person.

General H. Norman Schwarzkopf

"Stormin' Norman" Schwarzkopf became a familiar media personality as commander of the coalition forces during Operation Desert Storm in 1991. Ironically, the general, a decorated Vietnam War veteran, took orders from draft deferment king Dick Cheney who was then the secretary of defense. After the war, Schwarzkopf resisted the call to enter politics and instead published his autobiography, *It Doesn't Take a Hero*, for which he received a hefty advance. In the run-up to the Iraq War in 2003, Schwarzkopf urged caution and advocated for the United Nations weapons inspectors to be given more time to complete their task. He also correctly predicted "chaos" for the postinvasion occupation force and expressed alarm at then–Secretary of Defense Donald Rumsfeld's bellicose pronouncements: "He almost seems to be enjoying it."

William D. Geerhart

Gen. Norman Schwarzkopf
400 N. Ashley Drive
Number 3050
Tampa, Florida 33609

November 9, 1998

Gen. Schwarzkopf,

My son Billy asked me to send the enclosed letter to you as part of a project for school. I am writing this accompanying letter in the event that you have difficulty reading his handwriting.

He is a history buff and enjoys collecting Desert Storm cards. If at all possible he would like you to sign the attached card. Billy is a big fan of all your accomplishments and it would mean more to him than you could ever know. I must say I would get a kick out of it myself.

He is also running for his third grade class presidency and would like you to wish him luck. This entire enterprise is also part of a school project to write to a public official.

I appreciate you taking the time to consider this request. I realize you are quite busy. I am enclosing a self-addressed and stamped return envelope for your convenience.

Sincerely,

William D. Geerhart

GENERAL H. NORMAN SCHWARZKOPF

[FUN FACT]

Schwarzkopf's cuddlier nickname is "the Bear"—a term that has a different meaning in gay subculture. Don't ask, don't tell.

Northeastern University

College of Arts and Sciences
Department of Political Science

December 11, 1998

Dear Billy:

Thanks so much for your letter. You may be on the verge of a great political career. The first office for which I ever ran and won was as president of my third grade class! You, too, may become a governor and run for the presidency!

I am enclosing an autographed picture for you. Good luck in the election, and come back to Brookline and visit.

Sincerely,

Michael S. Dukakis

Mr. Dukakis sure seems lonely.

P.S. I teach at UCLA in the winter, so have your dad give me a call at the School of Public Policy, and drop in and say hello.

→

Michael Dukakis

The former governor of Massachusetts and Democratic nominee for president was destroyed by George H. W. Bush in 1988. Lee Atwater, architect of Bush's sleazy campaign strategy and a mentor to Karl Rove succeeded in linking the hapless governor to convicted killer Willie Horton, who had committed a brutal rape and assault while on a state prison furlough two years earlier. The Democratic candidate's implosion was not all attributable to the Republicans, however. Indeed, Dukakis's ridiculous photo op in a tank and his emotionless response to a debate question about his wife's hypothetical rape and murder helped seal his electoral fate. The defeated governor received an apology from a repentant and gravely ill Atwater shortly before the latter's death from a brain tumor in 1991.

303 Meserve Hall
Northeastern University
Boston, Massachusetts 02115
617-373-2796 (office) 617-373-5311 (fax)

© Marc Peloquin

Colin Powell

This Vietnam War hero, national security adviser to President Reagan, and chairman of the Joint Chiefs of Staff became President George W. Bush's marginalized secretary of state in 2001. Powell's service in the second Bush administration is mainly remembered for the dramatic, but largely fictional, case for the Iraq War that he delivered to the United Nations Security Council weeks before the invasion. The still widely admired moderate Republican's endorsement of Barack Obama in 2008 inspired scathing rebukes from the right wing, most vocally from recovering OxyContin addict Rush Limbaugh.

GENERAL COLIN POWELL

Gen. Powell only sent the card—he wasn't ready to offer a formal endorsement of Little Billy.

HOUSE OF COMMONS
LONDON SW1A 0AA

FROM THE PRIVATE SECRETARY TO
THE RT. HON. JOHN MAJOR, MP

18 December 1998

Dear Billy,

On behalf of Mr Major, I am writing to thank you for your letter asking him to sign the card you enclosed.

As you can imagine, Mr Major receives many requests of this kind and I am afraid therefore it is not possible for him to sign individual items sent to him. However, I enclose a photograph signed personally by Mr Major which comes with all his best wishes.

Yours sincerely,

L. Roper-Caldbeck

MISS LORNE ROPER-CALDBECK

Billy Geerhart

John Major or his assistant still has Little Billy's Desert Storm card, and he wants it back!

John Major

The uninspired prime minister of Britain from 1990 to 1997, and high school dropout, rose to serve in Margaret Thatcher's cabinet and succeeded her in office. In his postgovernment years, in addition to downplaying old scandals (at one point an old extramarital affair was made public), he has indulged his love of the game of cricket and has become a well-paid public speaker. In 2005 Major was knighted by Queen Elizabeth II.

November 29, 1998

Dear Mr. Reed,

This is a project for school. We are supposed to write to a person we admire and ask a question and get a letter back. I am running for third grade class president. I am promising longer recess and cheaper chocolate milk. I was wondering if you could give me some slogans? I would also like a signed picture. Thank you for your help. My teacher helped send this.

Sincerely,
Billy

Ralph Reed

This weasely political strategist is best known as the boy genius behind televangelist Pat Robertson's Christian Coalition. Early in his career Reed sought to establish a hardball reputation, but his prepubescent appearance and overreaching bravado worked against him. In 1991, for example, he told a newspaper reporter (who presumably resisted the urge to laugh): "I want to be invisible. I do guerrilla warfare. I paint my face and travel at night. You don't know it's over until you're in a body bag." In 2006 when his financial ties to power lobbyist and convicted felon Jack Abramoff were publicized, it was Reed who was in a body bag. As a result of the Abramoff association, the ersatz choirboy's campaign for lieutenant governor of Georgia didn't even make it past the primaries.

CENTURY STRATEGIES

January 28, 1999

Billy Geerhart

Dear Billy:

Thank you for your letter of November 29, regarding your campaign for third grade class president. I was involved in student politics as well and served as President of the Student Council in junior high school, so I know very well what you are undertaking.

I think a good potential slogan for your campaign might be something like "You deserve a voice!" When I was involved in student campaigns I always tried to promote myself as their voice before the administration, principals and teachers. Good luck to you! I hope this is the beginning of a great "Republican" political career.

At your service,

Ralph Reed, Jr.
President

RR/lbi

[FUN FACT]

In 1983 Reed was accused of plagiarizing part of a University of Georgia student newspaper column trashing the film *Gandhi* and was kicked off the publication.

November 29, 1998

Dear Mr. Russert,

This is part of a project for school. We are supposed to write a public person and ask a question and get a letter back. I am running for third grade class president. I need slogin ideas and my Dad said you used to work in politics. He is helping me mail this to you. I am running with promises of longer recess and cheaper chocolate milk. Could you also send me a picture wishing me luck?

Thank you,
Billy Geerhart

Tim Russert

The longtime host of the NBC news program *Meet the Press* employed a balance of avuncular good humor and prosecutorial zeal to frequently trip up even the most seasoned politicians. Russert, a Buffalo, New York, native and lawyer by training, served as chief of staff to Senator Daniel Patrick Moynihan and later as special counsel to Governor Mario Cuomo before transitioning into journalism. His sudden death in 2008 from a heart attack was mourned for days throughout the news industry and political world.

Little Billy was glad he used Tim Russert's slogan because he thinks he would have lost the election if he had gone with Ralph Reed's wimpy suggestion.

To Billy,
Good luck in your campaign!
Tim Russert
1998
Cheaper chocolate milk forever!

To Billy Geerhart with best wishes,

G— Bush

George H. W. Bush

This former president presided over the end of the Cold War and the feel-good Operation Desert Storm before losing reelection to a relatively unknown young governor from Arkansas. Ironically, it took the two-term presidency of Bush's eldest son to make his own four years in office look dignified and restrained by comparison. In retirement the man nicknamed Poppy likes to jump out of airplanes and hang out with his Oval Office successor and unlikely best friend, Bill Clinton.

GEORGE BUSH

March 1, 1999

Dear Billy,

This note is belated, but I did want to congratulate you on your selection as president of your third grade class. I know your dad is very proud of you.

As president of your class, Billy, you have a responsibility to be an example to the rest of your classmates. I'm sure your father has told you the same thing. Obviously, you already are showing some of the traits that are necessary to be a "leader" – honesty, loyalty, fairness, and compassion, to name just a few. I know you take your position seriously, and I wish you well.

Here's a photo of another president who hopes your future is bright and happy.

Sincerely,

G Bush

Billy Geerhart

Poppy Bush's kinder, gentler note was like a thousand points of light for Little Billy.

[FUN FACT]

He once called Al Gore "Ozone Man."

my

owr

wh

my f

und

IS t

bac

rents are letting me choose my
religion, could you please tell m
s cool about being ma
end Eddie says you
wear an
t f

[Religion]

4.

August 13, 2001

Dear Archbishop,
My parents have allowed me to choose
my own religion. Could you tell me
what's cool about Catholics? My
friend Eddie says you drink
blood which sounds pretty cool.
Please write me back because
I have to tell my parents my
decision.

Thanks,
Billy

Roman Catholic Church/
Cardinal Roger Mahony

This religion is known for its long-winded masses, strict parochial-school faculty, and rhythm-method approach to birth control. In 2007 the Los Angeles Archdiocese headed by Cardinal Mahony settled with 508 victims of clergy sexual abuse for $660 million.

Little Billy is glad he dodged that bullet.

Archdiocese of Los Angeles

Office of
the Archbishop
(213) 637-7288

3424
Wilshire
Boulevard

Los Angeles
California
90010-2241

September 6, 2001

Billy Geerhart

Dear Billy:

This is to acknowledge your recent letter of August 13, 2001 to His Eminence, Cardinal Mahony. The Cardinal wanted you to know that he enjoyed reading your letter.

Since choosing a religion is important in one's life, Cardinal Mahony is happy that you are investigating a number of religions prior to making your decision. Of course he is very pleased that you chose to write to him about Roman Catholicism.

You seemed particularly very interested about "blood". When Catholics go to church on Sunday we receive the Eucharist, which is the Body and Blood of Jesus. We believe that ordinary bread and wine are changed into the Body and Blood of Jesus by the prayers of the priest and the people.

I hope that this helps you in making your decision about what religion you will wish to follow. Cardinal Mahony would like you to discuss your decision with your parents. If you would like to learn more about the Catholic Church, Cardinal Mahony has kindly suggested that you and your parents go to a Catholic Church close by to where you live. He is confident that your questions will be answered there.

Once again, thank you for writing to Cardinal Mahony.

Sincerely yours,

Paul M. Albee

Reverend Monsignor Paul M. Albee
Secretary to the Cardinal

ENCLOSURE

cp

Pastoral Regions: Our Lady of the Angels San Fernando San Gabriel San Pedro Santa Barbara

August 13, 2001

Dear Sir,
my parents are allowing me to
choose my own religion. My friend
Eddie says your religion is
the easiest. IS that true?

Thank You,
Billy Geerhart

Presbyterian Church

This Christian faith began in the sixteenth century during the Protestant Reformation and
derives much of its heritage and many of its beliefs from the French theologian John Calvin
(1509–1564). The modern incarnation of the church is characterized by dependably short
services (usually no more than an hour), a conscientious clergy, and little if any guilt. In short:
the perfect low-maintenance religion.

GENERAL ASSEMBLY COUNCIL

PRESBYTERIAN CHURCH (USA)

Billy Geerhart

September 14, 2001

Dear Billy,

Thank you so much for your letter. I think it is great that you are learning about religions so that you can select one that's right for you. Religion is a very important choice because life is not always easy. There are good things and bad things that happen to us in life, and our religion helps us because we know that God loves us no matter what happens.

You would be very welcome in a Presbyterian church. It is an easy religion in that we ask that you love God with all your heart, soul, and mind, and that you love everyone as you love yourself. We ask that you say and believe that Jesus Christ is Lord and Savior, and seek to serve Him and follow His example each and every day. Your letter has made us think very hard about what it means to be a Presbyterian. Thank you for that.

A Presbyterian church that is close by you is the First Presbyterian Church of Hollywood. Their pastor is Alan Meenan. I have sent a copy of your letter and this letter to Rev. Meenan. I hope that he will be in contact with you soon.

Please come to a Presbyterian church. Bring your parents. Bring your friend Eddie. They'll be glad to see all of you.

Sincerely,

Kathy McMullen Lueckert

Kathy McMullen Lueckert
Deputy Executive Director
General Assembly Council

c: Rev. Alan J. Meenan
        First Presbyterian Church of Hollywood
        1760 North Gower
        Hollywood, CA 90028

Hare Krishna Hare Krishna Krishna Krishna Hare Hare Hare Rama Hare Rama Rama Rama Hare Hare

Iskcon ~ New Dvaraka

in service to Srila Prabhupada

August 15, 2001

Billy Geerhart

Dear Billy,

You are most fortunate that your parents are letting you *choose* your own religion, and you are even more fortunate in that you have inquired as to what is "cool" about Kṛṣṇa consciousness.

Kṛṣṇa consciousness is the original religion of the universe. It was given to the creator, Lord Brahmā, by God Himself in His form of Śrī Nārāyaṇa before the universe was engineered. Besides being the most authoritative, oldest, and most scientific process of religion known to mankind, it is also easily and joyfully performed.

Honestly speaking, all religions on the planet are or should be saying basically the same thing. Religion means to obey the word or laws of God. Just as in different countries there may be specific driving codes or laws which differ from one another, yet the basic principle of observing the traffic laws is universal. Similarly, there may be so many different rituals and rites for each and every religion, but the basic principle is to obey the laws of God. Now let us understand religion from another aspect or viewpoint.

Take for example, Mathematics. One starts off with basic arithmetic, then algebra, then geometry, then trigonometry, then calculus and so on. Each and every one of these branches is simply dealing with the numbers 0 thru 9, but each one is more advanced in concept than the preceding one. Similarly, there may be so many different religions in the world, but Kṛṣṇa consciousness is considered the post-graduate or highest knowledge of the science of God known to man to date. Kṛṣṇa consciousness teaches that God is ultimately the Supreme Person, Kṛṣṇa, Who is situated in your heart, and Who is the most

Sri Sri Rukmini-Dvarakadhisha Mandir
International Society for Krishna Consciousness - Founder Acharya His Divine Grace A.C. Bhaktivedanta Swami Prabhupada
3748 Watseka Ave., Los Angeles, CA 90034 PH: (310)839-1572 FAX: (310)839-2715

Hare Krishna

This religious group is dedicated to the worship of the Hindu god Krishna and known for their spirited chanting, airport evangelism, and killer vegetarian buffets. Former Beatle George Harrison helped mainstream Krishna mantras in his 1970 hit single "My Sweet Lord." The faith has been satirized in so many different films that the "Hare Krishna cameo" has become something of a tired cliché.

beautiful, most opulent, most intelligent, most powerful, most famous, and most renounced person anywhere to be found. The very name "Kṛṣṇa" signifies that He is all-attractive.

Kṛṣṇa consciousness teaches that the goal of life is to develop love of God on a most personal level. This is effected simply by chanting God's holy name in terms of the specific prayer or mantra known as the Mahā-mantra or the Great Chanting for Deliverance

Hare Krishna Hare Krishna, Krishna Krishna, Hare Hare
Hare Rāma Hare Rāma, Rāma Rāma, Hare Hare

Kṛṣṇa consciousness teaches that one can worship or love God moment by moment simply by dedicating and offering whatever one does, eats, says, thinks, etc. to Kṛṣṇa. Everything becomes a sacrifice or offering to God. One does not even need to do so in a temple, church or mosque. One can worship God anywhere provided the secret ingredient of love is present. If God is a person, then love is natural and easy, but if God is viewed as impersonal or void, then the natural flow of love is impossible.

Along with this letter is an introductory book which will help you to understand better what is Kṛṣṇa consciousness. If you have any further questions you can write to me at this address, or email me <nirantara@juno.com>.

Kṛṣṇe matir astu (may your mind be fixed on Kṛṣṇa)

Nirantara Dāsa
Director of Membership & Nāma-Haṭṭa

Little Billy's father was wondering whether the hot blonde on the cover of the Krishna booklet ever wound up being deprogrammed.

On Chanting HARE KRISHNA

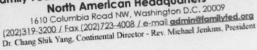

Family Federation for World Peace and Unification
North American Headquarters
1610 Columbia Road NW, Washington D.C. 20009
(202)319-3200 / Fax (202)723-4008 / e-mail admin@familyfed.org
Dr. Chang Shik Yang, Continental Director - Rev. Michael Jenkins, President

Master Billy Geerhart

Friday, August 24, 2001

Dear Billy,

Thank you very much for your beautiful letter. Unfortunately, Rev. Moon is out of the country right now. So he asked me to answer your letter the best I can.

My Name is Rev. Jorg Heller, but my friends all call me Yorg. I am the Executive Director of the "Family Federation for World Peace and Unification." Whoa! That is a long name, but that is what our Church is now called. It used to be called the Holy Spirit Association for the Unification of World Christianity. Also a very long name, but I liked it. The name suggests that we have world level goals, and we really do. We also called our Church the UNIFICATION CHURCH, because we want to bring all people together into one family.

What is cool about our Church? I think the coolest thing about us is that we have very strong families. When we get married (we call it actually "when we get blessed") we promise our spouse that we will love them for eternity, or forever, not "until death do us part." I am sure that you know already that when our life here on earth ends, we go to the Eternal World, the Spiritual World where we live forever.

There we can meet out parents and grandparents and all of our relatives and friends that have gone to the Spirit World before us.

Unification Church, aka the Moonies

This religion was founded in South Korea in 1954 by the Presbyterian-raised Reverend Sun Myung Moon. Church doctrine holds that a "sinless savior" or Messiah will save the world and form a kingdom of God on earth. In 1992 Moon surprised no one by unveiling himself as that Messiah. The church, which is known for its bizarre mass weddings and aggressive recruitment efforts, has frequently been called a cult with members referred to as "Moonies" for their extreme devotion to the founder.

We prepare ourselves well for our eternal life in the Spiritual World. We learn to love everyone, regardless of their nationality, race, or color of skin. One of our mottos is to "live for the sake of other's." It is very challenging and it takes some practice to give up one's selfish desires and put other's desires ahead of one's own. But the more you practice, the better you get and the more God is giving back to you.

The most unselfish being is God himself. He used all his energy to make this Universe. He did not hold anything back. And even though many people hurt God and are mocking Him, He still keeps on giving and loving even those people. Can you imagine how hard that must be? Jesus also said in the Bible to love your neighbor as yourself and even to "love your enemy." This is not an easy thing to do.

Is there anyone in your class or school that you really do not get along so well? I hope not, but if there is, try to think of something you could do that would make that person happy and than do it. Now that is really challenging, but God does that all the time. I try to do that also, but I fail sometimes. It just is very difficult to love someone that is not so nice to you.

If you grow up to learn to love people that seem to be unlovable, and give of yourself to the world without counting what you have given and without expecting anything back, then you become a real son of God. That is just what Jesus did.

Please look after your parents well. They really love you, even though they seem to give you a hard time sometimes. And please love your grandparents too. If they are still in this Physical World, I hope that they can stay in your house with you and your parents until they go to the Spirit World. God would just love that and they would too.

I am not sure if I am answering your question here, but I hope that this will give you some understanding what my Church is all about and what type of a person our pastor, the Reverend Sun Myung Moon is. I learned so much from him.

Anyway, Billy, if this brings up some more questions, you can write me again. I hope that I will be able to respond to you a bit quicker the next time.

I hope that you had a good summer vacation. Are you ready to go back to school? I have a son that is 10 years old and he really does not like to go back to school. Let me guess how old you are by studying your letter.

I think that you must be about 8 or 9 years old. I like your handwriting. You write very consistent and clear. Well, that is all for now.

God Bless you and your family,

Church of Satan

COS #365, Post Office Box 390009 San Diego, CA 92149-0009

We were established in 1966 c.e. by Anton Szandor LaVey, our High Priest, who declared the Year One, thus opening the floodgates to a revolution designed to smash the hypocrisy and unreason which has reigned for the past 2000 years. Though Dr. LaVey passed away in October of 1997, he instructed Blanche Barton, his long-time consort, to carry on as High Priestess. We have, since 1966, stood as the most formidable threat to those who would halt progress in the name of spirituality. We are explorers on the untrodden paths of science, human motivation and mystery—all that is most truly occult.

Those who proudly carry our cards identifying themselves as members have the strength and dedication to implement the tools of Satan, the imagination to confound and confuse, the wisdom to recognize the Unseen in our society, and the passions of a classical Romantic soul.

We don't solicit memberships; however, if you wish to join us, to show your support or appreciation, you can become a Registered Member. For a one-time registration fee of one hundred dollars, you will receive an embossed crimson card declaring you a member of the Church of Satan. No further dues will be expected. You'll also receive a questionnaire.

Filling out the questionnaire indicates your more serious interest in our organization. Once you complete and return it, your file will be reviewed for further involvement. We have affiliates/special interest groups of all persuasions who are working on many fronts toward the fulfillment of our Satanic destiny.

If you're anxious to have a more active part in furthering our cause, and feel yourself qualified, request information on becoming a Grotto Master. If accepted as a Grotto Master, this will give you the authority and training necessary to form your own Satanic grotto or group. If you already have an informal group going, applying for Grotto Master status is the perfect way to get official recognition and support.

We encourage each Satanist to take it upon himself to clear up misunderstandings of our religion wherever he sees them. You don't have to be part of a grotto to speak as a Satanist; you need no authority beyond being offended by stupidity and hypocrisy. Understand that if you wish to speak as a member of the Church of Satan, you are legally required to be a Registered Member. In addition, don't misrepresent yourself as being a spokesperson for the Church unless you achieve that status. But you can always defend Satanism as an avowed Satanist, proud of your religion.

If you have not already done so, we strongly suggest you purchase The Satanic Bible and study it. It is a diabolical book, the basis for our philosophy. Satanism is not for everyone, but if it is for you, we welcome you. We are not a fan club, a pen-pal society, or a lonely hearts group. We are a group of dynamic individuals who stand forth as the ultimate Underground alternative, the Alien Elite. We realize what we have, what we are, and what we shall become. Our scope is unlimited, and the extent of your involvement is based upon your own potential. All names and addresses are held in strict confidence and you are under no obligation as a Registered Member, unless you choose to present yourself for further consideration.

Please use the form below for registration.

CHURCH OF SATAN
COS #365, Post Office Box 390009
San Diego, CA 92149-0009 U.S.A.

Please enroll me as a Registered Member of The Church of Satan. Enclosed is $100.00 in U.S. cash, check or M.O.

Name (Mr./Mrs./Miss) _____

Street _____

City _____

Zip (or other) Code _____ Country _____

Sponsor if any _____

$100.00 to join?! That's a lot of allowance money. There better be a human sacrifice!

Church of Satan

This faith was founded in 1966 by Anton Szandor LaVey with the mission of celebrating the Dark Lord as a "symbol of personal freedom and individualism." When the church was first starting out in San Francisco, it attracted a fair amount of media attention that LaVey exploited further by performing satanic weddings, baptisms, and even a funeral for a U.S. Navy man (LaVey consigned the sailor's soul to the devil while a military honor guard stood by with an American flag). In 1969 LaVey published *The Satanic Bible,* which is still in print (but not yet on Kindle). The founding High Priest went to Hell himself in 1997, but the church continues to this day under new, if less flamboyant, leadership.

August 13, 2001

Dear Sir,
my parents are letting me choose my own religion. Could you tell me what is cool about your religion? Please write me back.

Thanks!
Billy Geerhart

Back again, by popular demand!

The Cloven Hoof

The Official Bulletin and Tribunal Of the Church of Satan

Under Blanche Barton's editorship, this Bulletin includes Satanic profiles, pertinent news, events, articles, new LaVeyan releases and rip-offs, fiction, movie and book reviews, sociological, anthropological, and mesozoological follies, poetry, applications and analyses of pursuits Magical and Mundane. It will also serve as a much-needed mobilization communique, enabling speedy response from our Satanic forces.

If you've had a great idea for a short essay swimming around in your head, some Satanic news we should all know about, if you know of a haunted or mysterious place in your area that other Satanists would be interested in, if you've been baffled and bemused by the latest urban legend or ridiculous talk-show topic, or misuse of the English language on the airwaves, now's your time to shine! Send any short articles, thoughts, suggestions—and your request for the current issue, to Miss Barton today.

Note: No full subscriptions are available at this time, but a current single copy is only $5, plus mailing cost (U.S.: $1.25. Canada: $1.50. Mexico: $2. All other countries: $4).

The Cloven Hoof
COS #365, Post Office Box 390009
San Diego, CA 92149-0009 U.S.A.

Please send a current single copy of **The Cloven Hoof** to:

Name and address:

[FUN FACT]

LaVey was the technical adviser on the 1975 horror film *The Devil's Rain* starring William Shatner and Ernest Borgnine. He also played the role of the high priest.

Dear friend,

Hello – and thank you for your interest in American Atheists!

This brochure, *INTRODUCING AMERICAN ATHEISTS,* will give you a brief idea of what Atheism, and our organization, are about. It will provide you with a brief overview of some of our activities, including our efforts to make our voices heard in the nation and various state legislatures, as well as in preserving our heritage through the Charles B. Stevens American Atheist Library & Archives.

American Atheists is the oldest continuously operating national organization for Atheists in the United States. It grew out of the historic *MURRAY V CURLETT* (1963) US Supreme Court case which helped to end forced prayer and Bible-verse recitation in the taxpayer-supported public schools. American Atheists was the first to host a national convention for Atheists; it was also the first openly Atheist group to have representatives testify before a committee of the US Congress. We organized the first "Atheist Pride" marches, the first national Atheist television program, and much more.

As President of American Atheists, it has been my task to lead the organization into its latest stage of development – and into the next millennium. This means providing Atheists with a professional, articulate voice in state capitals across the country – and in Washington, DC, as well – to deal with issues which affect Atheist civil rights and the separation of state and church. It also means educating the public about Atheism as a positive, life-affirming philosophy.

You can help, by joining American Atheists and supporting this work – work which is really for you. Help by adding your voice in the effort to advance reason, freedom, and the separation of state and church!

For Reason and the First Amendment,

Ellen Johnson

ELLEN JOHNSON, President
AMERICAN ATHEISTS

Little Billy was astonished to learn that there was once prayer in public schools. He is very grateful to Ms. O'Hair for her sacrifice.

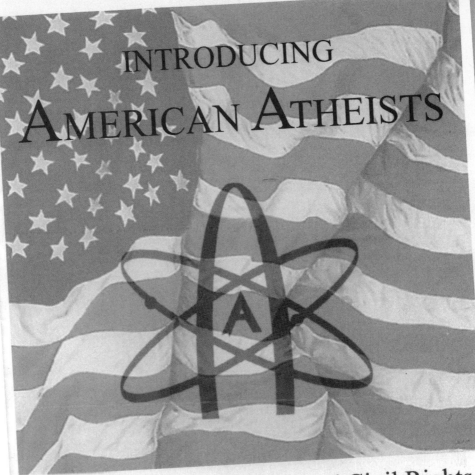

INTRODUCING

AMERICAN ATHEISTS

Leading the Way for Atheists' Civil Rights
and the Separation of Church and State

American Atheists

This nonprofit organization dedicated to the separation of church and state was founded in 1963 by Madalyn Murray O'Hair, the person *Life* magazine once called "America's most hated woman." The rabble-rousing O'Hair started American Atheists in Austin, Texas, after winning a landmark Supreme Court case that effectively ended prayer in public schools. In 1995 O'Hair and two family members were abducted and later murdered as part of an elaborate robbery scheme carried out by a former employee of American Atheists and two accomplices. The organization continues today under more sedate management, and in 2002 organized the Godless Americans March on Washington. The event attracted slightly fewer people than the average Catholic funeral.

August 13, 2001

Dear Sir,
My parents have allowed me to
choose my own religion. Could
you tell me whats cool about
your religion? My friend
Eddie says you like aliens
and volcanos which sounds
cool! Please write me back!

Thanks,
Billy

THE
FIRST
BOOK
ON
OPERATING
THETAN

Church of Scientology

This is the controversial, celebrity-courting religion founded by science fiction writer L. Ron Hubbard in 1954. The founder left the mortal plain in 1986 to continue his work in an "exterior state," but the faith continues under equally loopy management. Adherents to Scientology pay for educational materials, courses, and counseling or "auditing" sessions that involve a device called an E-meter that allegedly measures the electrical responses of the subject. The goal of dedicated Scientologists is to attain a state of "clear" in which troubling memories in the "reactive mind" are eradicated. The most committed, deep-pocketed parishioners ascend to a special level in the church in which they are treated to some mediocre Hubbard fantasy pulp (or "scripture") concerning an evil alien overlord named Xenu and volcanoes. Thanks to public records from Scientology court cases and the Internet, the entire Xenu creation myth has been widely disseminated—most memorably in a 2005 *South Park* episode.

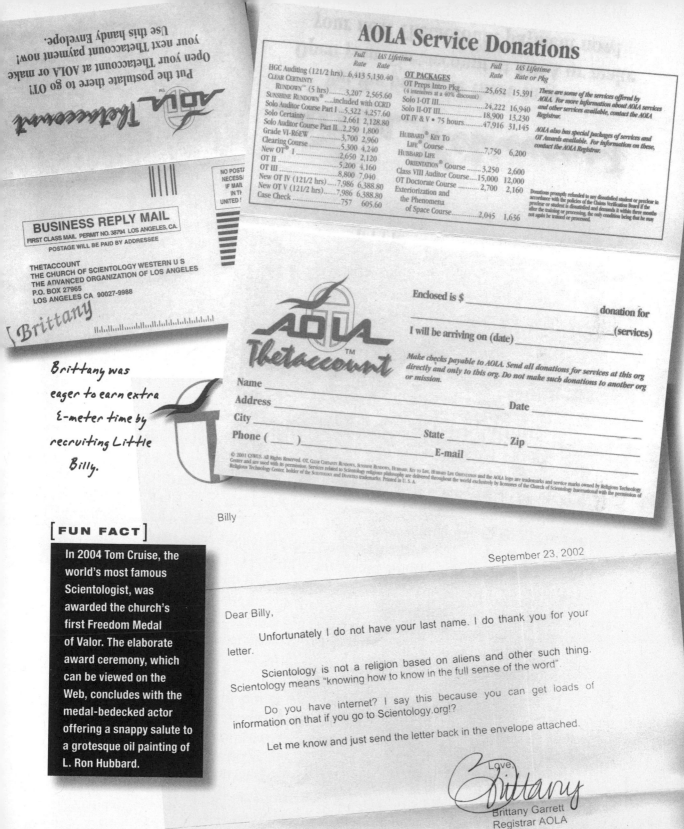

AOLA Thetaccount

BUSINESS REPLY MAIL
FIRST CLASS MAIL. PERMIT NO. 38794 LOS ANGELES, CA.

POSTAGE WILL BE PAID BY ADDRESSEE

THETACCOUNT
THE CHURCH OF SCIENTOLOGY WESTERN U S
THE ADVANCED ORGANIZATION OF LOS ANGELES
P.O. BOX 27965
LOS ANGELES CA 90027-9988

[*Brittany*]

NO POSTAGE
NECESSARY
IF MAILED
IN THE
UNITED STATES

*Brittany was
eager to earn extra
E-meter time by
recruiting Little
Billy.*

AOLA Service Donations

	Full Rate	IAS Lifetime Rate		Full Rate	IAS Lifetime Rate or Pkg
HGC Auditing (12 1/2 hrs)...	6,413	5,130.40	**OT PACKAGES**		
CLEAR CERTAINTY RUNDOWN™ (5 hrs)...	3,207	2,565.60	OT Preps Intro Pkg. (4 intensives at a 40% discount)...	25,652	15,391
SUNSHINE RUNDOWN®...included with CCRD			Solo I-OT III...	24,222	16,940
Solo Auditor Course Part I...	5,322	4,257.60	Solo II-OT III...	18,900	13,230
Solo Certainty...	2,661	2,128.80	OT IV & V • 75 hours...	47,916	31,145
Solo Auditor Course Part II...	2,250	1,800			
Grade VI-R6EW...	3,700	2,960	HUBBARD® KEY TO LIFE® Course...	7,750	6,200
Clearing Course...	5,300	4,240	HUBBARD LIFE ORIENTATION® Course...	3,250	2,600
New OT® I...	2,650	2,120	Class VIII Auditor Course...	15,000	12,000
OT II...	5,200	4,160	OT Doctorate Course...	2,700	2,160
OT III...	8,800	7,040	Exteriorization and the Phenomena of Space Course...	2,045	1,636
New OT IV (12 1/2 hrs)...	7,986	6,388.80			
New OT V (12 1/2 hrs)...	7,986	6,388.80			
Case Check...	757	605.60			

These are some of the services offered by AOLA. For more information about AOLA services and other services available, contact the AOLA Registrar.

AOLA also has special packages of services and OT Awards available. For information on these, contact the AOLA Registrar.

Donations promptly refunded to any dissatisfied student or preclear in accordance with the policies of the Claims Verification Board if the preclear or student is dissatisfied and demands it within three months after the training or processing, the only condition being that he may not again be trained or processed.

AOLA Thetaccount

Enclosed is $ _____ donation for
_____ (services)

I will be arriving on (date) _____

Make checks payable to AOLA. Send all donations for services at this org directly and only to this org. Do not make such donations to another org or mission.

Name _____
Address _____
City _____   Date _____
Phone (___) _____
State _____ Zip _____
E-mail _____

[FUN FACT]

In 2004 Tom Cruise, the world's most famous Scientologist, was awarded the church's first Freedom Medal of Valor. The elaborate award ceremony, which can be viewed on the Web, concludes with the medal-bedecked actor offering a snappy salute to a grotesque oil painting of L. Ron Hubbard.

Billy

September 23, 2002

Dear Billy,

Unfortunately I do not have your last name. I do thank you for your letter.

Scientology is not a religion based on aliens and other such thing. Scientology means "knowing how to know in the full sense of the word".

Do you have internet? I say this because you can get loads of information on that if you go to Scientology.org!?

Let me know and just send the letter back in the envelope attached.

Love,
Brittany
Brittany Garrett
Registrar AOLA

Dear Billy,

My name is Ricky Roehr and I am the president of the US Raelian Religion. I hope that it is OK with you that I replied to your letter to Rael. Rael has given me permission to write to you, and hopes that you understand. ☺

Thank you for writing to the Raelian Religion. Your parents obviously love you very much since they are letting you choose your own religion. This is one thing that Rael was taught by The Elohim (the extraterrestrials that created all life on earth) – to respect children and treat them as the individuals they are and to let them discover and search for their own religion and to respect their individuality. You are lucky to have parents like this !

Are you on the internet? If you are, you can look at the Raelian Religion website www.rael.org. Maybe you have already seen it and this is perhaps why you wrote to Rael?

The Raelian Religion is, for me, the most wonderful of all religions. Like you, I searched for several years before choosing a religion for myself. Do you already know that only about 20% (1/5) of the people on earth are Christian? That means that there are almost 5 BILLION people that believe in something different than most people in the USA ! That's a lot of people don't you think ? The Raelian Religion recognizes not only Jesus, Moses and the prophets of the Bible, but all the prophets of the earth. Buddha, Joseph Smith, Mohammed….many… … because many prophets were sent by Our Creators. (these people that came from another planet) As Raelians, we respect all beliefs and would never try to convince you or anyone else that our religion is right. If we did this, it would mean that we do not respect your right to choose for yourself.

When I was your age, it never made sense to me that people would argue or even start wars just because one religion claimed to be better than another religion. It seemed crazy to me that everyone was praying to the same "God" But arguing that one religion was right, and another wrong. I thought there was a god at this time because my parents told me there was. Now I believe that we were created by *people* that came from another planet – just like our scientists on earth are beginning to discover how to create life. They created us mastering the science of DNA technology. Maybe you have heard of DNA in school. If you have not heard of it yet, you will soon.

To answer your question "what is cool about our religion?" To me the cool things are that we are responsible for all of our actions... or even lack of action if we should have taken action. Another thing is that we are all free (like your parents are teaching you!) to choose our own paths in life. Another thing that is very special to me is that by living "responsibly" (not hurting anyone, not judging anyone, never making anything that is living to suffer etc) we can live without feeling guilty. And the most important thing is something that every prophet tried to teach humanity, to love ourselves more so that we can love others more.

I will be happy to answer any questions you may have. Write me if you like and I promise to tell Rael all about your letter.

Respectfully,

Ricky Roehr
4601 Green Canyon Dr
Las Vegas, Nv 89103
Rroehr1946@aol.com

[FUN FACT]

Bishop Boisselier, the clone queen, is married to Ricky Lee Roehr, the enthusiastic Raëlian who wrote to Billy.

Raëlism

This Paris-based UFO religion was founded in the 1970s (of course) by a former French sports-car journalist and test driver named Claude Vorilhon (aka Raël). Adherents to the faith believe that Raël received special knowledge and instruction from space aliens called the Elohim. Raëlians also believe that ancient visitation to the Earth by the Elohim inspired many of the world's major religions. In 2002 Raëlian "Bishop" Brigitte Boisselier announced that her Raëlian-backed company, Clonaid, had successfully birthed a human clone named "Eve." To date there has been no evidence to substantiate this claim.

William D. Geerhart

President Thomas S. Monson
Church of Jesus Christ of Latter Day Saints
50 W. N. Temple St.
Salt Lake City, Utah 84150

February 15, 2002

Dear President Monson,

Enclosed please find a letter from my son. My wife and I are encouraging his spiritual curiosity and right to choose his own beliefs.

It would me a lot to him if you would write him back directly. I have given him permission to open any mail that is addressed to him.

Thank you for taking the time to consider this request. Please do not take offense at my son's questions as he is just curious about the world and hears a lot of things from a variety of sources.

Kindest Regards,

William D. Geerhart

The Church of Jesus Christ of Latter-Day Saints, aka the Mormons

This religion was founded in 1830 by Joseph Smith, Jr., and based on scripture engraved on "golden plates" conveniently buried near Smith's home in western New York. A friendly angel named Moroni allegedly guided the founder to the holy dishware, and Smith translated the engravings into the Book of Mormon, the foundation of the faith. Another angel—this one with an attitude and a drawn sword—supposedly forced the practice of polygamy on the vision-happy leader. Smith embraced the concept with gusto and took at least thirty wives before being killed by an angry mob in Illinois in 1844. Aside from the plural marriage thing (officially renounced by the church in 1890), Mormons are known for their temple garments (aka magical underwear), vicarious baptisms, and extremely persistent missionaries.

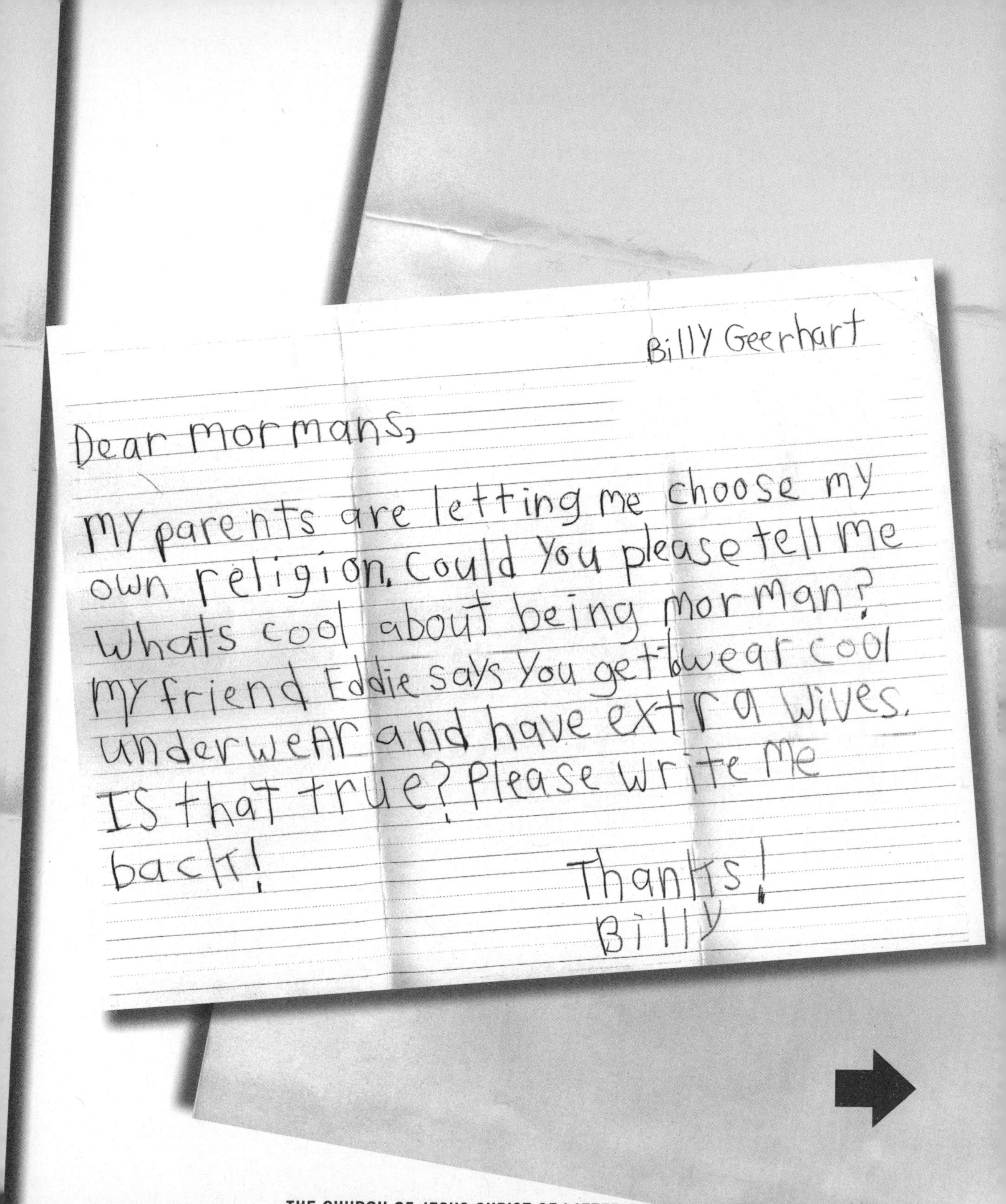

Billy Geerhart

Dear mormans,

My parents are letting me choose my own religion. Could you please tell me whats cool about being morman? My friend Eddie says you get to wear cool underwear and have extra wives. Is that true? Please write me back!

Thanks!
Billy

THE CHURCH OF JESUS CHRIST OF LATTER-DAY SAINTS
OFFICE OF THE FIRST PRESIDENCY
47 EAST SOUTH TEMPLE STREET, SALT LAKE CITY, UTAH 84150-1000

February 20, 2002

President T. Dean Christensen
California Los Angeles Mission
1591 East Temple Way
Los Angeles, CA 90024-5801

Dear President Christensen:

I have been asked to forward to you the attached copies of correspondence addressed to President Thomas S. Monson from William Geerhart and his son Billy. Billy has several questions concerning the Church.

Would you please ask that missionaries meet with this young man and his parents. President Monson is confident that Billy will be able to make the correct decision as he meets with the missionaries who have been asked to make a personal visit, and as he earnestly seeks the truth. Please provide this office with a report of the visit.

I have been asked to extend the best wishes of the Brethren as you preside over the California Los Angeles Mission.

Sincerely yours,

F. Michael Watson
Secretary to the First Presidency

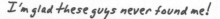
I'm glad these guys never found me!

Remarkably, there was only one occasion where flesh-and-blood reality intruded on Billy's carefully constructed fictional world. One evening two Mormon missionaries showed up unannounced at the Geerhart residence in Los Angeles and asked to meet with their potential young recruit. The fact that the author's apartment was littered with beer bottles and pizza boxes and decorated with Cold War–era posters did not dissuade the enthusiastic evangelizers from believing that a child (and a *wife*) lived there. The presence of a disheveled *male* roommate didn't set off any alarm bells for them either. In fact, the dogged religious salesmen returned several more times before finally being told that Billy and his mother had moved away on the spur of the moment to become Catholics. The author is looking forward to finding out what Mormon hell looks like.

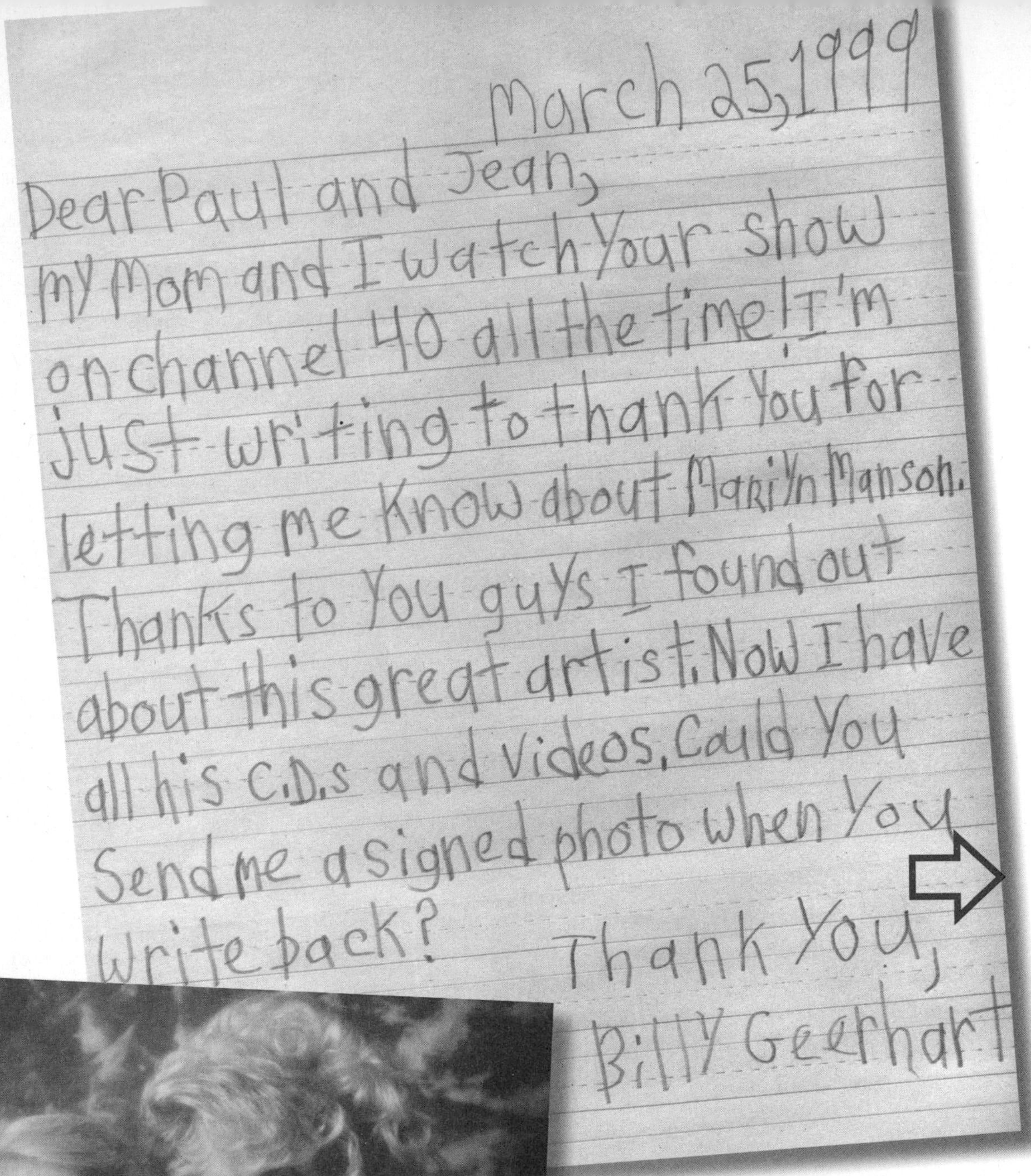

March 25, 1999

Dear Paul and Jean,

My Mom and I watch your show on channel 40 all the time! I'm just writing to thank you for letting me know about Marilyn Manson. Thanks to you guys I found out about this great artist. Now I have all his C.D.s and videos. Could you send me a signed photo when you write back?

Thank you,

Billy Geerhart

April 15, 1999

Dear Billy,

We were pleased to receive your letter. We feel especially complimented when young people write us because it shows us they're interested in the important things in life. Many young people are so busy trying to have fun and make their way in the world that they have no time to think about where they will spend eternity. This life is "even a vapour, that appeareth for a little time, and then vanisheth away." (James 4:14) One poet described it this way:

Only one life
'Twill soon be past.
Only what's done for Christ
Will last.

We assume you have invited Christ into your heart and are trying as best as you can to live for Him. You know, Billy, God has a plan for your life, and it's the best thing that could ever happen to you. It does, however, require something from you--your life! Your best! Your all! In asking your all, God also gives you Himself and is always your best Friend--one that sticks closer than a brother.

Life isn't easy for the youth of today. They have much pressure at school and at their jobs to go with the crowd. Satan can make the way of the ungodly crowd look so glamorous and inviting, but the end of that way is destruction, for Satan comes only to steal, kill and destroy.

We are so glad you are a part of TBN! That is an encouragement to us. Remember to read the Word daily, praying always for the Holy Spirit to guide you.

Sincerely in Christ,

Paul C. Jan

Trinity Broadcasting Network • International Headquarters
2442 Michelle Drive, Tustin, CA 92780

Paul and Jan Crouch/
Trinity Broadcasting Network

This Christian television power couple founded the Southern California–based Trinity Broadcasting Network (TBN) in 1973 during a brief partnership with the up-and-coming Jim and Tammy Faye Bakker. After some ugly internal business struggles, the Bakkers left for their own well-known soap opera in North Carolina. TBN is now the largest Christian TV network in the United States, but its leadership hasn't exactly been scandal-free. In a 2000 suit that was ultimately settled out of court, Paul Crouch was accused of plagiarizing his end-times novel and film *The Omega Code*. In another, more significant embarrassment, the *Los Angeles Times* reported in 2004 that Crouch had paid a former male employee $425,000 to settle a sexual harassment suit.

Wh
bes
Mo
I g

arents said I can gamble
n I get older. What is the
game to play to g...
y for a ...

5.

[Vices]

July 22, 2001

Dear Flynt,

My parents said I could subscribe to your magazine when I turn 18. That is a long time from now. My friend Eddie asked me to ask you if there is a Hustler for kids that wouldn't make my parents mad. Please let me know. Thank you!

Billy

Larry Flynt

A self-described "smut peddler who cares," Flynt made his name as the founder and publisher of the explicit *Hustler* magazine in the 1970s. The man who has a fondness for American-flag diapers has also become a free-speech hero to some for the many obscenity trials he has fought to keep his publication on the newsstands. It was during such a trial in 1978 that Flynt was shot and paralyzed from the waist down. A white supremacist claiming to be outraged by an interracial photo layout in *Hustler* confessed to the attack but has never been charged. The unrepentant pornographer's most famous First Amendment triumph was over Jerry Falwell, who had filed a libel suit against *Hustler* for a satirical advertisement that depicted the Moral Majority founder as having lost his virginity to his mother in an outhouse. Falwell ultimately lost his case in a landmark Supreme Court ruling, but surprisingly, later became friends with his old nemesis. In recent years Flynt has performed the valuable public service of exposing the hypocrisy of insufferable government moralists/adulterers like Senator Bob Livingston and Senator David Vitter.

Larry Flynt

July 26, 2001

Billy Geerhart

Dear Billy,

    Your parents are right. You can subscribe to Hustler when you turn 18. Hang in there - you'll be 18 before you know it. Until then, you should read the Sears & Roebuck catalog.

Sincerely,

Larry Flynt

Larry Flynt

LF:rrw

[**FUN FACT**]

Flynt claims to have had sex with a chicken when he was nine.

Angeles Executive Office • Beverly Hills, California 90211 • Phone 323-651-5400 FAX 323-651-0488

Dear Mr. Groom,
My parents said I can gamble when I get older. What is the best game to play to get enough money for a speedboat? Could I get some chips from you?

Thanks!
Billy

The Original Caesars Palace

This Las Vegas gambling paradise was inspired by the opulence and excess of ancient Rome. The Palace, which first opened its doors in an extravagant ceremony in 1966, was the brainchild of businessman Jay Sarno, who once explained that there was no apostrophe in "Caesars" because he believed every guest was a king. In 1967 motorcycle daredevil Evel Knievel successfully jumped the ornate fountains outside of the hotel but had a rough landing and spent the next twenty-nine days in a coma.

Office of the President

3570 Las Vegas Boulevard South
Las Vegas, Nevada 89109
Main: 702-731-7110
Direct: 702-731-7300
Fax: 702-731-7307

January 28, 2002

Master Billy Geerhart

Dear Billy:

Thank you for your letter. You have asked me a very difficult question, because some people who gamble lose their money instead of buying a speedboat.

Gambling is a form of entertainment like going to a movie.

The best way to get a speedboat is to do well in school, so that when you are grown up, you will be smart enough to earn money to buy your own boat.

And if you decide to gamble when you are old enough and can afford it, I recommend betting the pass line in the game of dice. Your money will last longer and hopefully you will have a lot of fun before the casino's mathematical edge claims your last bet.

Hope this letter helps. Good luck to you in school.

Sincerely,

John Groom
President

JG/ls

Dear Mr. Busch, Aug, 13, 2001
My Parents told me I can start
drinking beer when I turn 21.
That is a long time from now!
Could you tell me if there is a
beer for kids? If there is not
could you tell me how much beer
will cost in the future?
I want to start saving now.
                    Thanks!
                    Billy Geerhart

Anheuser-Busch Companies, Inc.

Now owned by the Belgian beer conglomerate InBev, Anheuser-Busch was founded as a Bavarian Brewery in St. Louis, Missouri, in 1852. The company owns a number of different beer brands including Budweiser, the brew endorsed by Bud Man, the alcohol-loving superhero dreamed up by marketers back in the late 1960s.

ANHEUSER ✦ BUSCH
Companies

Francine Katz
VICE PRESIDENT
CONSUMER AFFAIRS

August 28, 2001

To the Parents of:
Billy Geerhart

Dear Mr. and/or Mrs. Geerhart:

Your son sent us the enclosed letter, and I am directing my reply to you since it is our policy not to correspond with children on issues relating to our adult products.

I have enclosed our 2000 annual report so that you can go through it with your son and answer any questions he may have regarding our company. In addition to our commitment to producing quality products, Anheuser-Busch is also committed to seeing that our products are used responsibly and by adults. With the help of experts in the child psychology field, our "Family Talk About Drinking" program was developed to help parents talk to and educate their children about underage drinking. I have enclosed a copy for your use.

On behalf of Anheuser-Busch, thanks for your interest and best wishes for the upcoming school year.

Sincerely,

Francine I. Katz

*Little Billy should have written
directly to Bud Man. Bud Man
would have answered his questions
without tattling to the
'rents.*

One Busch Place • St. Louis, Missouri 63118-18

family talk

How to talk
to your kids
about
drinking

ANHEUSER-BUSCH COMPANIES, INC. 97

A Guide for Parents

Sorry for the delay
in getting back to you
Billy. We are buried in
thousands of letters

[Career Advice]

March 17, 1998

Dear Mr. Greenberg,

This is a project for my school. We are supposed to write to a company we would like to work for someday. Could you give me some pointers on what to study to improve my chances of getting hired? Also — do workers get free McNugets? Just so you know — my first choice of a job is with 7-11.

Thanks,
Billy

McDonald's Corporation

The quintessential American fast-food restaurant was founded by Dick and Mac McDonald in San Bernardino, California, in 1940 but was built into a franchise behemoth by Ray Kroc. The corporation now counts 30,000 restaurants in 119 countries. McDonald's targeted, kid-friendly advertising has introduced generations of children to the wonders of high-calorie processed food as well as to morally questionable characters like the burger-looting Hamburglar and the initially "evil" shake-stealing Grimace.

THANK YOU

Thank you for your interest in McDonald's.

We are pleased to send you the enclosed material.

If you have any further questions,

please write or call us at:

McDonald's Customer Satisfaction Department

One Kroc Drive

Oak Brook, Illinois 60521

(630) 623-6198

Cordially,

Beth Petersohn

Beth Petersohn,

Manager, Customer Satisfaction Department

Printed on Recycled Paper

McDONALD'S

This annual report did not live up to its cover.

McDonald's Corporation

Performance At A Glance

WENDY'S INTERNATIONAL, INC.

R. DAVID THOMAS
Senior Chairman of the Board & Founder

April 13, 1999

Mr. Billy Geerhart

Dear Billy:

Thank you for your complimentary letter. I am glad that some day you would like to work for Wendy's. In regard to your questions concerning some advice on becoming an employee. You mentioned your desire to succeed. Honesty is very important in any business. That is part of the advice I give to anyone who asks for the secret of success. The other part is hard work and integrity. If you have these qualities, Billy, and have that desire to succeed, there isn't any reason why you would not be successful.

I have enclosed an article written about Wendy's and me. I believe it will answer some of your questions. I have also enclosed some coupons for you to use on your next visit to Wendy's, as my guest. Enjoy!

Good luck with your future endeavors.

Sincerely yours,

R. David Thomas

RDT:rh
Enclosure

Wendy's Founder Dave Thomas

Like many high school dropouts, Dave Thomas worked in the fast-food industry as a teenager. Unlike most dropouts, Thomas became filthy rich. He fell in love with the business early on and forged a bond with mentor Colonel Harland Sanders of Kentucky Fried Chicken fame. A turning point in Thomas's career came when he reversed the fortunes of four failing Kentucky Fried Chicken restaurants and sold them back to the corporation, making himself a millionaire by the age of thirty-five. He opened the first Wendy's restaurant in Columbus, Ohio, in 1969, naming it after one of his daughters. Contrary to popular belief, the portly hamburger mogul died in 2002 of liver cancer, *not* a Biggie Sized heart attack.

4288 WEST DUBLIN GRANVILLE ROAD, DUBLIN, OHIO 43017 TELEPHONE (614) 764-3100

Starbucks Coffee Company
P.O. Box 34110
Seattle, WA 98124-1110
206/447-1575

Howard Schultz
chairman and
chief executive officer

Little Billy's mother likes the
Venti Java Chip Frappuccino,
which sounds like a triple
Nesquik for grown-ups.

March 29, 1999

Billy Geerhart

Dear Billy,

Thank you very much for your nice letter. You and your classmates are very wise to begin planning now for your future.

My suggestions for study would include computer classes because the Internet is rapidly changing our traditional ways of doing business. I'd recommend taking English and writing classes because that will give you an edge over others who find it difficult to speak and write their thoughts and ideas. I also think it's important that you study something that *you* enjoy doing, such as making art or playing music, or being involved in a favorite sport. And probably most important of all, remember to always be respectful and considerate of people and their feelings.

Best of luck to you.

Howard Schultz

Starbucks

The ubiquitous coffee-shop colossus is famous for having introduced Italian phrases to lowbrow Americans and providing shelter for homeless screenwriters. The first store opened in Seattle in 1971, but it took marketing genius Howard Schultz, who came along in 1982, to transform the chain into the caffeinated juggernaut it is today.

march 18, 1999

Dear Mr. Drexler,
This is a project for school. We
are supposed to write to a company
We'd like to work for some day. Could
you give me some pointers on
what to study to improve my chances
of getting a job working for one of
your stores? I am good at shirt—
folding. Just so you know — 7-11
is my first choice for a job.
Thank you,
Billy Geerhart

The Gap

This clothing store chain is known for its omnipresent shirt-folding salespeople, celebrity
ads, and offshoots babyGap and GapKids. The first unassuming Gap store was opened in San
Francisco, California, in 1969 by founders Donald and Doris Fisher. There are now over 3,000
stores worldwide, including one unlikely outlet in Iran.

Millard S. Drexler
President
Chief Executive Officer

One Harrison Street
San Francisco, CA 94105
650 952 4400 tel

Gap Inc.

Gap
Banana Republic
Old Navy

March 31, 1999

Mr. Billy Geerhart

Dear Billy:

Thank you for choosing us for your letter writing project. We're glad that we're the kind of company you'd like to work for some day.

The best way to learn about this business is to spend some time working in our stores. You can apply for part-time or summer work when you turn 16.

I'm enclosing one of our limited edition T-shirts, which we had specially made. Enjoy -- and thanks again for writing.

Sincerely,

This watch, which came with the T-shirt and other swag, broke two days after Little Billy got it.

:mme

march 18, 1999

Dear Mr. Davenport,

This is a project for school. We are supposed to write to a company We would like to work for someday. Could you give me some pointers on what to study to help me get hired? I'd like to work at the counter. What happened to the Colonel? Just so you know— I would also like to work at 7-11.

Thank you,
Billy Geerhart

KFC

The fast-food chain known for its delicious buckets of artery-clogging fowl was first franchised as Kentucky Fried Chicken in 1952 but rebranded to the more benign "KFC" in 1991. The company founder and mascot, Colonel Harland Sanders, earned his honorary military rank in 1930 courtesy of the governor of Kentucky in recognition of his culinary contributions to the Bluegrass State. The Colonel received a final salute upon his death in 1980 when his southern gentlemanly attired remains lay in state in the rotunda of the Kentucky State Capitol. Sanders has since been resurrected in KFC advertising as a peppy cartoon character.

March 25, 1999

Mr. Billy Geerhart

Dear Billy:

Thank you for your letter and your kind words about KFC. It is always gratifying to hear from our customers and to know we are putting smiles on so many faces because of our delicious meals.

I thought you might be interested in some comments of our CEO who was recently asked questions about developing a career and motivation.

-- Learn to write as well as you possibly can. (He has a journalism degree which he believes is key to many careers.).

-- KFC is inspiring because, next to the U.S. military, it is one of the most integrated workforces.

-- Admirable traits: Energy, enthusiasm, talent.

-- Favorite quote: <u>Mark Twain:</u> "I was born excited." Always be positive.

-- Here at KFC, we believe in "assuming innocence". For instance, if you are counting on a co-worker to give you a report on Monday and he doesn't have it on your desk, we are encouraged to first believe there must be a very good reason why he could not do the report, rather than be angry and demand an explanation. This strategy promotes an atmosphere of trust, respect and good manners.

Of course, our founder, Col. Harland Sanders, was well-known for his business integrity and determination. He used to say "A man will rust out faster than he will wear out". He lived to be 90 years old and was actively involved in our company until the last few weeks of his life. He believed in staying busy and actively sought rewarding activity every day. I'm enclosing some material about this inspiring man.

I hope you are having a great school year.

Sincerely,

Shirley Topmiller
Shirley Topmiller
Public Affairs Department

enclosure

This guy looks just like the ghost of my Grampa Jim, but without the shotgun.

From Corbin to the World

BIRTHPLACE OF KENTUCKY FRIED CHICKEN

The following articles are reprinted from a 1980 issue of KFC's publication commemorating the 50th anniversary of the founding of

march 11, 1999

Dear Rev. Jentzch,

This is a project for my school. We are supposed to write to a company we would like to work for some day. My friend Eddie says you have a Navy with cool uniforms. How could I join and what should I study to get in? Just so you know — my first job choice is 7-11.

Thanks,
Billy

P.S. Eddie helped me send this to you.

Heber Jentzsch/Scientology

Reverend Jentzsch's sensitivity about his religion being called a "company" is understandable, because for decades the Internal Revenue Service classified Scientology as a commercial enterprise. In 1993, however, the lawsuit-weary government agency surrendered and reinstated the church's coveted tax exemption, thus legitimizing it as a religious institution. In its desperation to end the church's relentless pressure campaign, the IRS apparently overlooked the fact that most religions don't have special branches in which people dress up in navy-type uniforms and sign billion-year contracts of service.

CHURCH OF SCIENTOLOGY INTERNATIONAL

REVEREND HEBER C. JENTZSCH
President

Billy Geerhart

March 25, 1999

Dear Billy,

Thank you for your letter. Maybe your friend Eddie doesn't know we are a Church not a company. A very small percentage of Scientologists wear the Navy type uniform as in its forming stage certain members worked aboard a fleet of ships.

When you are of age and have completed your schooling you are welcome to come and see what we do and find out if you would like to be part of our Church. Then, if your parents approve, you can join us and start working for the Church.

I am sending you a little booklet called The Way to Happiness which is a non-religious moral code based on common sense which you may find useful.

Wishing you success with your studies.

ML

Heber Jentzsch

WOOD BLVD., SUITE 1200, LOS ANGELES, CA 90023 · 6329
PHONE: (323) 960-3500 FAX: (323) 960-3508/09

The Way to HAPPINESS
A COMMON SENSE GUIDE TO BETTER LIVING

TO: BILLY GEERHART
" HEBER C. JENTZSCH

June 17, 1999

Dear Mr. Kennedy,

This is a project for my school, for extra credit in our unit on jobs we can write to people and ask a question. My friend Eddie said you have a really cool, easy job. Could you tell me what to study to get a job like yours? Just so you know my first choice is 7-11 because they have video games. Do you get to play video games? Please also send a picture.

Thanks,
Billy

Patrick J. Kennedy

While some said it couldn't be done, in seven short terms Patrick Kennedy, a Democratic congressman from Rhode Island and the son of the late senator Edward Kennedy, has more than lived up to the daunting family tradition of erratic behavior in office. Among other obnoxious feats, the young lawmaker has honored the dark side of Camelot by crashing his Ford Mustang into a Capitol Hill barricade in 2006, pitching a fit at an airport security guard in 2000, and boasting in a speech to the Young Democrats organization in 2003: "I have never worked a f***ing day in my life."

PATRICK J. KENNEDY
1ST DISTRICT, RHODE ISLAND

WASHINGTON OFFICE
312 CANNON HOUSE OFFICE BUILDING
(202) 225-4911
FAX: (202) 225-3290

DISTRICT OFFICE
249 ROOSEVELT AVENUE, SUITE 200
PAWTUCKET, RI 02860
(401) 729-5600
(800) 392-5772
FAX (401) 729-5608

NATIONAL SECURITY COMMITTEE
RESOURCES COMMITTEE

MEMBER
PORTUGUESE-AMERICAN CAUCUS
NEW ENGLAND CAUCUS
ITALIAN-AMERICAN CAUCUS
FRIENDS OF IRELAND
OLDER AMERICANS CAUCUS
LAW ENFORCEMENT CAUCUS

Congress of the United States
House of Representatives
Washington, DC 20515

Billy Geerhart

July 2, 1999

Dear Billy:

Thank you for your letter. I appreciate hearing from the young people like yourself from around the country. Right now is a good time for you to begin thinking about your future.

I learned at a young age that I wanted to go into public service. Many of my family members worked for the government. My uncle, John F. Kennedy, was President of the United States and my father, Edward Kennedy, is a senator from the state of Massachusetts. I saw what they were doing for other people and wanted to do something similar.

In order to achieve my goal becoming a public servant, I went to Providence College after I graduated from high school. While I was still in college, I was elected to be a State Representative. When I was 26, the people of the first district of Rhode Island elected me to be a United States Representative.

Your friend Eddie was partially right about my job. It is very rewarding, but also very difficult. However my job allows me to do things that I truly enjoy. I get to meet wonderful people and travel all over the world. I also enjoy reading and playing sports, especially tennis and swimming. Doing all of those things do not leave much time to play video games.

To get a job with which you will be really happy, it takes a lot of hard work. I would encourage to study hard in school and get involved with your school and your town. I am including a biography on my life and a picture. I hope you enjoy them. I wish you the best of luck for the future.

Sincerely,

Patrick J. Kennedy
Patrick J. Kennedy
Member of Congress

Amway Corporation • 7575 Fulton Street East • Ada, Michigan 49355-0001

DICK DEVOS
President

Amway

May 19, 1999

Billy Geerhart

Dear Billy:

{ This famous global direct-selling company was founded in 1959 and uses multilevel marketing to sell beauty, nutrition, and home-care products. Because of the overzealous nature of Amway's layered sales recruitment and the motivational fervor of many so-called Amwayians, the company has often been accused of being a cultish pyramid scheme. A 1979 ruling from the Federal Trade Commission deemed the company to be a legal enterprise, but ordered it to cease misrepresenting earnings, sales, and profits to recruits. Richard DeVos, Amway's billionaire cofounder, is known for owning the Orlando Magic basketball team and managing to get a heart transplant at the unlikely age of seventy-one. His son, Dick, was president of Amway from 1995 to 2002, after which he spent millions of his own money in a failed bid to become the Republican governor of Michigan in 2006.

Thank you for your recent letter. I am happy to learn that you are thinking of working for Amway Corporation when you grow up. Although, I don't know how we can compare to your first-choice employer, 7-Eleven. We don't have too many video games available to our employees at their workstations! *What's a "workstation"? Sounds awful!*

I hope that you continue to apply yourself in many areas of study throughout your school years. There are many skills that will be needed in the workplace of the future. Basic math and English skills are most important because they will help you with more advanced skills such as computer technology and communications. These skills will be even more important as the business world continues to advance technology. We have many areas within Amway that require specialized skills including our Marketing, Finance, Purchasing, Research & Development and Computer System Divisions.

I wish you well in your remaining school years. You have a lot of adventure and learning ahead of you!

With warmest regards,

Dick DeVos
President

DDV/ak

kinko's

Kinko's, Inc. ■ Corporate Office
P.O. Box 8000
255 West Stanley Avenue
Ventura, California 93002-8000
TEL (805) 652-4000

March 23, 1999

Billy Geerhart

Dear Billy:

Thank you for your interest in working for Kinko's. I am flattered that Kinko's is one of your choices for a job, and I am very happy to tell you that we were selected as one of the 100 Best Companies to work for in America. This award is a great recognition for all of the co-workers in our company who work to take care of our customers.

When you are just starting off on a career search like you are, it is very important to study hard and to take pride in the grades that you earn in your classes. As you become older, you can apply your work ethic and good study habits to courses that will teach you about business and to courses that will teach you about people.

At Kinko's, we value good knowledgeable co-workers who are people oriented and treat our customers like guests in our branches.

I hope this helps you, and I want to wish you good luck in your studies.

Sincerely yours,

Joe Hardin, Jr.
Chief Executive Officer

JH:le

P.S. Your printing is very good!!

Kinko's

This famous copy-shop business was founded in 1970 by Paul Orfalea, whose nickname is "Kinko" because of his curly hair. Orfalea opened the first Kinko's near the University of California at Santa Barbara, where the store presumably benefited from high-volume left-wing-student political-flyer copying. The chain was acquired in 2004 by Federal Express, and by 2008 the corporation had begun a rebranding effort to change the name on its 1,500 locations to FedEx Office. Regardless of the company name, the copy outlet will always be home to frantic, caffeine-addled people trying to finish something.

More than 850 Kinko's locations worldwide. For the location nearest you, call 1-800-2-KINKOS or visit our web site at http://www.kinkos.com.

November 26, 1999

Dear Dr. Kevorkian,
My school project is to write to somebody
I like and ask a question. I want to
be either a doctor or a 7-11 clerk
because they have video games.
could you tell me the best way to
get to be a doctor like you?
Thank you, my brother helped
me find your address.
                              Sincerely,
                              Billy

Dr. Jack Kevorkian, aka Dr. Death

This eccentric crusader for physician-assisted suicide helped over 130 terminally or chronically ill people end their lives before being sentenced to twenty-five years in prison on a 1999 second-degree murder conviction. Dr. Kevorkian became an irresistible media presence during his heyday in the 1990s because he looked like an undertaker and often exhibited a dark enthusiasm for his controversial services. Kevorkian was paroled in 2007 for good behavior and because he agreed to the condition that he would not aid in any future mercy killings.

JUNE 9, 2001

DEAR BILLY,

My lawyer told me that I should not answer every letter I get, but I did especially like yours and passed it on to my legel assistant who now is working on a book.

In response to your question, sometimes I wish I was a 7-11 clerk!

It's nice to know that your father and brother are so helpful and caring.

Good luck with your future plans.

Sincerely,
Jack Kevorkian, MD

Ruth Holmes, CDE
President

Tel: 248-540-7026
Fax: 248-540-1225
E-mail: PentecInc@aol.com

Pentec, Inc.

Handwriting & Document Examiners

P.O. Box 204   Bloomfield Hills, MI 48303

Sorry for the delay in getting back to you Billy. We are buried in thousands of letters, but Dr. K loved yours! Good Luck! Ruth Holmes

Sorry for the delay in getting back to you Billy. We are buried in thousands of letters, but Dr. K loved yours! Good Luck! Ruth Holmes

APRIL 6, 1999

To Whom It may concern,
This is a project for school. We are
supposed to write to companies we
might like to work for some day. I was
told your company is cool. What should
I study to get hired? Just so you know
my first choice is 7-11 because
they have video games. Do you
have video games?

Thanks,
Billy

RAND

April 7, 1999

Billy Geerhart

Dear Billy:

RAND does not have video games. But we are cool. If you would like to work for
RAND you should study very hard. Be sure to work hard in math and science.

Good luck!

Amanda Gaylor
Public Information
310-451-6913
amanda_gaylor@rand.org

*What's so cool about working
hard in math and science? Is
she trying to be funny?*

The Rand Corporation

The Santa Monica, California–based global policy think tank was started in 1946 by the U.S. Army Air Forces as Project RAND (the name is derived from "Research and Development") under a contract to the Douglas Aircraft Company. In 1948 it separated from the military and became a nonprofit entity with a mission to "help improve policy and decision making through research and analysis." Because of the organization's military roots and its significant influence on government, especially during the Cold War, RAND is frequently mentioned in various conspiracy theories.

CATO

April 30, 1999

Billy Geerhart

Dear Billy:

It is great that you are already planning ahead for your future. The best thing you can do now for yourself is to do your best everyday with all your school work. You will use all of your subjects later in life.

We have many opportunities at the Cato Institute for bright achievers of every discipline. English class is important because it helps you speak and write properly. Good communication skills will enable you to excel wherever you choose to work. Science is also beneficial because it offers explanations for the mysteries of life. It also helps you think critically. Good math skills will assist you throughout your life. Art class could also lead to very practical and enjoyable work in your future.

If you like video games, you may also like computer programs and computer graphics. Our Web site designers have put together an interactive and visually pleasing Web site at www.cato.org.

The best thing you can do for yourself is to discover the subjects you enjoy the most. Remember, if you work hard today, the world will open up to you tomorrow.

Best Wishes,

Patricia E. Mohr
Patricia E. Mohr
Public Affairs Assistant
Cato Institute

Cato Institute • 1000 Massachusetts Ave., N.W. • Washington, D.C. 20001 • (202) 842-0200 • FAX: (202) 842-3490

The Cato Institute

This libertarian, nonprofit think tank is headquartered in Washington, D.C., and was founded in 1977. The institute derives its name from eighteenth-century essays that were named after Cato the Younger, defender of republican institutions in ancient Rome. Cato hands out something called the Milton Friedman Prize each year to universal indifference.

National Hobo Association
P.O. Box 706
Nisswa, MN 56468

Mr. Billy G...

July 26, 1999

Dear Hobos,

This is a project for my school.
We are doing a special unit on
careers. We are supposed to write
to someone who has a job we like.
My first choice of a job is 7-11 but
If that does not work I'd like to
be a Hobo. Could you tell me what I
should study to become a good
Hobo

Thank you,
Billy

LAUREL NEBEL
9502 N.E. 13TH STREET
BELLEVUE, WA 98004
(425) 454-6886

August 6, 1999

Dear Billy's Parents,

Your son wrote The Hobo Times saying he wanted to work at the 7-11 or be a hobo. The Editor of the Times read me his letter this morning and it was a tickle. The enclosed novel is for 10 to 90 year-old adventure lovers. I don't know your son's age, but if you feel it's a book he'd be interested in and it's age appropriate please give it to him. I think he'll really like it.

"The Iron Road Home" does not glamorize hoboing. As you are aware riding the rails is dangerous and the book spells out the dangers of riding freight trains. The story is of a gone-by era, when hoboes were hard working honest men.

I hope you and your family enjoy the book.

Give Billy a hug for me, he sounds like a great kid!

Laurel Nebel
Laurel Nebel

118 P.S. If Billy likes the book and his friends want to buy a copy it can be order at your local book store. It's also available at: BARNESANDNOBEL.com & Amazon.com. Or they can send me $8.00 and I'll mail it to them.

Hobos

The origin of the term *hobo* is not 100 percent settled, but it started appearing in the 1800s when certain unwashed free spirits carrying sticks with attached bags started hopping railroad cars to get around the United States.

National Hobo Association

P.O. Box 706 • Nisswa, MN 56468 • 218-963-7557

August 23, 1999

Dear Billy,

Thank you so much for your fine letter. I hope I can answer your question.

You've asked me what you can study in school to become a good hobo. I should tell you right now that the word hobo does not describe a job or an occupation. No Billy, the word hobo describes a person who is curious about all things in life, is self confident in his or her ability to lead a meaningful life, is fascinated with traveling and seeing new places and most of all shows respect for all people. Hoboes believe in themselves and their future.

The hoboes throughout our history have had many jobs or occupations. They helped build the railroads when America was young, the worked as cowboys on the great cattle ranches out west, they worked on construction projects and they sailed the ocean ships. Most hoboes learned more than one trade or job. That way, they could be sure of finding a job wherever they traveled. Some were sign painters some worked in printing companies, some were farm workers and some worked in the mines. But they always believed in working for their food and shelter.

To prepare yourself for becoming a hobo when you're older I'd suggest that you practice being a good boy and respecting your parents, helping them whenever you can. If you have brothers or sisters help them and treat them with love as you would like to be treated. Also, be a good citizen... respect the law, don't lie or steal and have faith in the future. Be kind to those people who have less than you. Be kind to animals and respect our trees and nature. Learn to appreciate America for the great country she is. You live in the greatest country on earth where little boys can grow up to be a President, an astronaught, a scientist, a musician or poet or painter or anything else you set your mind to be.

As far as school work goes, you should first listen carefully to what your teachers tell you. Then, learn to read well. You can't learn anything if you can't read. Then read everything you can get your hands on, books, magazines and newspapers. Study the history of your state, our country and the world. You can't have a future if you do not understand the past. Don't be afraid to ask your teacher questions, insist on learning your lessons. Don't ever be a quitter, if you have trouble understanding your schoolwork, ask for help. When you grow up you'll be glad you did. If you do all the things I've suggested I'm sure the people at 7-11 would be proud to hire you.

Buzz Potter, Editor

Buzz Potter

Little Billy was impressed to learn that modern-day hobos are so damned proud and self-promotional.

April 22, 1999

Dear Mr. Mathews,

I wrote you a long time ago, my project is almost due and I wish you would write me back. My project is to write to a company we would like to work for someday. My first choice of a job is to work at the counter of 7-11. Could you give me some pointers on what to study so I will be hired? How old do I have to be? Do you have to be Indian to work there? My friend Eddie said that.

Thanks,
Billy

7-Eleven

The convenience-store behemoth evolved from the simple idea of a Southland Ice Company dockworker in Dallas, Texas, in 1927. The employee's concept of selling basic food items on Sundays and evenings when grocery stores were closed caught on and expanded into a chain called Tote'm. In 1946 Tote'm became 7-Eleven to reflect the chain's new extended hours of 7 A.M. to 11 P.M. Today most 7-Elevens are open 24 hours a day and are known for their endlessly rotating hot dogs, behind-the-counter porn magazines, and grainy surveillance-camera robbery videos.

THE
SOUTHLAND
CORPORATION

August 5, 1999

Clark J. Matthews, II
President and
Chief Executive Officer

Billy Geerhart

Dear Billy:

I hope you will accept my sincerest apologies for not writing to you sooner. Your letter states that you would like to work at 7-Eleven® someday. I think you have made an excellent choice because there are many employment opportunities at 7-Eleven when you become of age.

My suggestion to you would be to stay in school, learn as much as you can, and get your high school diploma. After you graduate from high school, you could apply at your local 7-Eleven store, or if you're interested, talk to our Human Resource Manager, Matt Reilly (714/529-7711), about our Store Manager Training Program. You do have to be 18 years of age to work in a 7-Eleven store.

Billy, thanks for taking the time to write me, and I wish you the best! As a token of our appreciation, please accept the enclosed Slurpee® coupons, Slurpee lapel pin, 7-Eleven night-light, 7-Eleven pen and pencil.

Good luck to you!

Sincerely,

Clark Matthews

Clark J. Matthews
President and Chief Executive Officer

Enclosures

You had me at Slurpee coupon!

STORE COUPON | EXPIRES DEC. 31, 2000

FREE SLURPEE®

Your choice of one 12oz. Slurpee frozen beverage, any flavor.

Offer good at participating 7-Eleven stores. Limit one coupon per customer per day. Offer not valid with any other coupon or discount. No cash value.

114454

7-ELEVEN 121

march 18,1999

Dear Mr. Brown,
This is a project for my
school. We are supposed to
write to a company we would
like to work for some day.
Could you give me some pointers
on what to study so maybe
I'll get hired? My Dad said he'll
teach me how to shoot when I
get older. Just so you know—
my first job choice is 7-11

Thank You,
Billy Geerhart

Pinkerton

America's oldest private security guard and detective agency was founded by Allan Pinkerton in 1850. The official history of the agency found on its company website trumpets such accomplishments as foiling an 1861 assassination attempt on President Abraham Lincoln and tracking down famous Wild West gangs. Not mentioned is Pinkerton's sometimes violent role in late nineteenth-century labor strikes and union spying. Today paranoid business executives can still hire Pinkerton agents as spies, but now they are called "undercover operatives."

WORLD SUPPORT CENTER
4330 PARK TERRACE DRIVE
WESTLAKE VILLAGE, CA 91361
TELEPHONE 818 706 5614
FACSIMILE 818 706 4919
E MAIL Denis_Brown@usa.Pinkertons.com

DENIS R. BROWN
PRESIDENT & CEO

PINKERTON®

March 26, 1999

Mr. Billy Geerhart

*I used this magnifying
glass to set my sister's
Barbie doll on fire. It
was so cool!*

Dear Billy:

Thank you for your letter to Mr. Denis Brown regarding future employment
at Pinkerton. The enclosed brochure describes different ways that Pinkerton
protects people and businesses. Jobs range from investigators to computer
technicians to security officers. In order to be able to train for the type of job
you would like, please make sure that you develop good reading, problem
solving and communication skills before you graduate from high school.

Thank you for considering a career with Pinkerton.

Sincerely,

Rebekah Davis Dillingham
Assistant to the President

Enclosures: Brochure
            Gift

7.

[Consumer Charity]

Dear Terr/
My Dad told
to put the
room so we c
He also said i
We'll set it up

May 12, 1999

Dear Mr. Smith,

I am writing to You because my Dad's old car is broken. Now we have to ride the bus with all the smelly people. I was wondering if You could give my family a big car like the one my teacher drives. It looks like this ↓

Please?

Thank You!
Billy

My brother found Your address.

General Motors

This once great symbol of American industry was founded in 1907 and filed for Chapter 11 bankruptcy in 2009. In the waning days of the Bush administration, the automobile giant received billions in government bailout money while it continued to manufacture the automotive atrocity known as the Hummer.

LORNA G. UTLEY
Director
Diversity Initiatives
    and Philanthropy

Public Policy Center

May 26, 1999

Mr. Billy Geerhart

Dear Mr. Geerhart:

Thank you for your letter to General Motors requesting the donation of a car like your teacher drives. We read your letter with interest and commend your personal dedication to your father's transportation problem.

General Motors receives numerous requests to provide support to individuals from a wide range of locations throughout the world. Most of these requests, like yours, are for deserving individuals with unique circumstances. Regrettably, due to the high volume of requests we receive for such support, our contribution guidelines preclude us from making donations to individuals.

We hope you will understand our position. On behalf of General Motors, please accept our best wishes.

Sincerely,

And Little Billy's family is still using public transportation.

General Motors Corporation
Public Policy Center

3044 West Grand Blvd.
Mail Code 482-111-134

Detroit, MI 48202-3071

313-556-3632
Fax 313-974-4451

GENERAL MOTORS   127

November 29, 1998

Dear Mr. Brennan,

My name is Billy and my family is very poor. We used to have an old Sears ice box (that's what my Dad calls it) but it broke. Now we really do have to use an ice box and buy ice every day. I was wondering if you could give my family a refrigerater? My DAD's name is William D. (Donald) Geerhart my brother is helping me mail this to you. We want to surprise my DAD.

Thanks, Billy

Circuit City

The electronics and appliance chain that began as Wards Company in 1949 went bankrupt in 2008 and liquidated its final store in 2009. The company now exists only as an online entity.

CIRCUIT CITY®

Circuit City Foundation
9950 Mayland Drive
Richmond, VA 23233-1464
(804)527-4000 (Ext. 4204)
FAX: (804)527-4173

January 6, 1999

Billy Geerhart

Dear Billy:

I am truly sorry to tell you that our company's and Foundation's policies prevent us from making grants of cash or merchandise to or for the benefit of individuals.

We wish your family every success in raising the funds you need to get a refrigerator. We wish we could have helped.

Yours truly,

C. Stoddart.

Cassandra O. Stoddart

COS:jg

Would it have killed them to send Little Billy a fridge during liquidation?

August 13, 2001

Dear Sir,

Could your company please give my family a jacuzi? We are too poor to aford. Please write me back.

Thank you,

Billy

Jacuzzi

The Jacuzzi hot tub, always a reliable symbol of a luxurious lifestyle, evolved from a humble submersible bath pump developed by Candido Jacuzzi in 1948 for his son, who suffered from rheumatoid arthritis. Candido was one of seven Jacuzzi brothers who immigrated to California from Italy in the early 1900s. It was a third-generation Jacuzzi named Roy, though, who gave the world the hedonistic product we all know and love today. The original brothers might not know what to make of some of the things that have taken place in the hot tubs that bear their universally recognized surname—especially in the 1970s.

JACUZZI® INC. World Headquarters

2121 N. California Blvd., Suite 475
Walnut Creek, CA 94596
(925) 938-7070 FAX (925) 938-0183

World-Wide Divisions:
Jacuzzi Whirlpool Bath
Jacuzzi Brothers
Jacuzzi Brazil
Jacuzzi Chile
Jacuzzi Europe
Jacuzzi UK Bathroom Products
Jacuzzi UK Kitchen Products
Jacuzzi Singapore
Jacuzzi Canada
Eljer Plumbingware
Bathcraft
Redmont
Sundance Spas
Atlantic Pool Products
Century Heating Products
Gatsby Spas

August 29, 2001

Billy Geerhart

Dear Billy,

My name is Terry Goss, and I work for Mr. Jacuzzi. He is away from our office just now, and he asked me to write to you in reply to your letter of August 13th. Mr. Jacuzzi is very interested in your request, but it is important for us to have some more information before we can give you an answer.

Could you tell me something about you and your family, such as how old you are, how many brothers and sisters do you have, and is there a particular reason you are looking for a Jacuzzi unit? Is this something you would put inside or outside for your family to use? Who would put it in and make it run?

There are some questions we would need to ask a grown-up in your family. Could you please tell me who we should talk to?

Billy, I will wait to hear from you. Please write soon.

Terry Goss

Terry Goss

This guy never wrote back or delivered the Jacuzzi. Maybe a celebrity needed it more.

September 9, 2001

Dear Terry,
My Dad told me to tell you he'd like to put the jacuzi in the living room so we can watch T.V. in it. He also said if you give it to us we'll set it up with hoses from the back of the house, Thanks! I can't wait!

Billy

[Morality Advice]

January 8, 1999

Dear Mr. Bennett,

My brother said I should write you with this question because you are moral and you know about drugs because you knew Janis Joplen (my brother said you would know what this means). Anyway, I saw my math teacher smoking a funny smelling cigaret before school last week. He was laffing at the chalkboard too. Should I call the F.B.I.? Please write back.

Thanks,
Billy

William J. Bennett

This perpetually grumpy conservative commentator was a Republican administration figure in the 1980s—he served as secretary of education under President Ronald Reagan and as the so-called drug czar under President George H. W. Bush. After leaving government, Bennett gradually built a profitable career as a professional moralist with his *Book of Virtues* series and *The Death of Outrage*—a literary scolding of the nation for not being more upset about Bill Clinton's character flaws. The morality gravy train derailed in 2003 when it was revealed that the virtue czar had a major gambling habit that had cost him millions over the years in Sin City.

WILLIAM J. BENNETT

Suite 900
1701 Pennsylvania Avenue, N.W.
Washington, D.C. 20006

April 12, 1999

Mr. Billy Geerhart

Dear Billy:

Thank you for your letter. I do not think that you need to call the F.B.I. about the matter regarding your teacher. Instead, you may want to discuss the incident with your parents or your school principal.

Sincerely,

William J. Bennnett

What a lame response, but at least he didn't send an autographed copy of The Children's Book of Virtues.

January 8, 1999

Dear Dr. Dobson,

My brother said I should write to you because you talk about morals on the radio. Last week at school I saw my drama teacher mr. Smoot kissing a man in shorts with a mustash. They were sticking thier toungs out at each other. It looked silly. Should I tell on them or is it o.k.? I am also in Mr. Smoot's play (the music man). Should I stay in the play? Please write me back soon. Thanks,

Billy

Dr. James Dobson

The evangelical psychologist and radio host founded Focus on the Family, a religious nonprofit organization "dedicated to nurturing and defending families worldwide" in 1977. Dobson, who is the author of the suggestively titled pro–corporal punishment book *Dare to Discipline*, once tried to link the cartoon character SpongeBob SquarePants to the "homosexual conspiracy." Shortly before the 2008 presidential election, Focus on the Family issued the dire *Letter from 2012 in Obama's America* that warned of the potential consequences of the Democratic nominee's first term in office. The document's author, "a Christian from 2012," informs the present-day undecided voter that among other things four American cities have been struck by terrorists, pornography is available on network television, and the Boy Scouts have chosen to disband rather than abide by a Supreme Court ruling allowing gay scoutmasters. If all these abominations happened in the hypothetical first term, the "Christian from 2016" must *really* be freaking out.

February 1, 1999

Billy Geerhart

Dear Billy:

Dr. Dobson was pleased that you took the time to write to him, and he's disappointed that he is unable to respond personally to you. He receives thousands of letters every day, so he has asked me to answer you for him. We hope you understand.

We're glad you felt comfortable sharing with us about your drama teacher, Billy. We can understand why you're feeling confused by his actions, and wondering how you should respond to what you saw. However, we're encouraged by your desire to do what's best in this tough situation, and we want you to know that we'll be praying for you this week, asking God to give you wisdom and guidance as you try to do the right thing. He knows all about what is happening, and He wants to guide you through this. That's why we encourage you to also pray about this problem. The Lord will hear and answer your requests as you trust in Him.

Having said that, we think the best thing for you to do is to talk with your parents about the things you told us. Ask them if they think you should stay in the play, because, ultimately, they're the ones who will make the final decision. You may also want to talk about your concerns with your Sunday School teacher or a Christian adult that you respect to get his or her thoughts. One reason that God has put these people in your life is to help you through situations like this one. For this reason, we believe they may have some valuable advice to share with you.

Thanks, again, for sharing with us, Billy. We hope you'll let us know if there's ever anything else we can do to help. God bless you as you look to Him in the days ahead.

Your friend in Christ,

Kristin Dale

Kristin Dale
Correspondence Assistant to Dr. Dobson

Dear Beverly,   January 8, 1999
My brother told me I should write
to you because you are a true
American. Last week my teacher
told our class that comunism
was good and if there is any justice
in the world the Red Tide will rise again
and swallow America (whatever that means). Is
this wrong of my teacher? My brother
said I should call the F.B.I. Please
write me back!

Thank you,
Billy

Beverly LaHaye

She is the founder of the conservative Concerned Women for America (CWA), an organization started in 1979 with the mission of "reversing the decline in moral values in our nation." In 1976 Beverly cowrote the libido-stifling Christian sex manual *The Act of Love* with her husband, Tim LaHaye, the bestselling author of the *Left Behind* series. Mrs. LaHaye, who touts herself as a "women's rights pioneer," more than earns that title with this quote from her feminist manifesto *The Spirit-Controlled Woman*: "Submission is God's design for women."

20 years of service
1979-1999

March 2, 1999

Billy Geerhart

Dear Billy,

Thank you so much for your recent letter to Concerned Women for America (CWA). I agree with you, Billy, Mrs. LaHaye is a true American. Thanks to her, here at CWA our mission is to protect and promote **Biblical values** among all citizens – first through prayer, then education, and finally by influencing our society – thereby reversing the decline in moral values in our nation.

Thank you again for writing. I encourage you to read the writings of the founding fathers of our nation; do not simply read what others say about them but read what they themselves wrote. Whenever you come to anything that you do not understand, ask your parents or your brother for help. God bless you, Billy.

Sincerely,

P. George Tryfiates
Executive Director

PGT/bp

CONCERNED WOMEN FOR AMERICA
1015 Fifteenth Street, N.W. • Suite 1100 • Washington, DC 20005 • 202-488-7000 • Fax 202-488-0806 • www.cwfa.org

BEVERLY LAHAYE 139

Dear Billy,   APRIL 14, 1999

    I received your letter to Mr.
milken and I sent it to ...
I know he'll be d...
receive it...
you s...

cla...
and...
boat...

[Billy-nomics]

9.

march 26, 1999

Dear Mr. Rubin,
I am writing to you for extra credit in my economics unit in Mr. Riggott's class. I want to ask you what is the fastest easiest way to save up enough money for a speedboat? I get $10.00 a week allowance and $20.00 a month helping my brother deliver newspapers. Please also send me a signed picture.
Thank You,
Billy

Robert Rubin

This Ivy League–educated deregulation champion and former Goldman Sachs executive served as President Bill Clinton's second treasury secretary. After his government service, Rubin became the well-compensated director and senior counselor at Citigroup and was, for a brief period, chairman. He quietly resigned from his position at the troubled financial institution in 2009 after helping to nurture its spectacular meltdown. That same year Rubin earned the Wall Street equivalent of the Razzie Award when he was named one of *MarketWatch*'s Ten Most Unethical People in Business.

DEPARTMENT OF THE TREASURY
WASHINGTON, D.C. 20220

June 30, 1999

Billy Geerhart

Dear Billy:

Thank you for your letter to Secretary Rubin. I am sorry it has taken so long to respond. We receive so much mail on the many issues for which the Treasury Department is responsible, we cannot reply as rapidly as we wish. I hope you understand and are still interested.

The Secretary is honored that you requested his autographed picture and asked that I forward the enclosed picture to you along with a copy of his biographical sketch. You also requested information about the fastest way to save enough money to buy a speed boat. It would not be appropriate for the Treasury Department to make specific recommendations regarding investments. Your best course of action would be to contact local banks or savings associations or a major securities dealers listed in your local telephone book. There are many safe investments that would pay you a satisfactory return on your money. I am sure that you will find one that will meet your needs.

Thank you again for writing to Secretary Rubin.

Sincerely,

Dale M. Servetnick
Deputy Director, Office of Public Correspondence
dale.servetnick@do.treas.gov
http://www.ustreas.gov/opc/

Enclosures

Little Billy is sure relieved he never got any financial advice from Mr. Rubin. Billy's also glad he doesn't have any Citigroup stock!

Robert E. Rubin

BOARD OF GOVERNORS
OF THE
FEDERAL RESERVE SYSTEM
WASHINGTON, D. C. 20551

April 8, 1999

Mr. Billy Geerhart

Dear Mr. Geerhart:

Chairman Greenspan asked me to thank you for your recent letter about your plans for saving money. A speedboat is an expensive item, and starting to save now is a great idea. The longer you have to invest your savings the better your return will be.

I have enclosed some pamphlets and a photograph of the Chairman.

Sincerely,

Lynn Fox

Lynn Fox
Assistant to the Board

Enclosures

ONCE UPON A DIME

FEDERAL RESERVE BANK
OF NEW YORK

Alan Greenspan

The former chairman of the Federal Reserve was nicknamed "The Maestro" by biographer Bob Woodward for his early jazz-music background and his steady hand on the economy. This rather grand sobriquet might also apply to Greenspan's improbable ability to score with network newswomen as he dated Barbara Walters in the 1970s and married NBC's Andrea Mitchell in 1997. His platonic pal, writer, and philosopher Ayn Rand had a more down-to-earth pet name for the dour economist: "The Undertaker." Greenspan received the Presidential Medal of Freedom from George W. Bush in 2005 presumably for endorsing his irresponsible tax cuts for the wealthy. And while The Maestro may have been only a breath away from the president when the highest civilian award was draped around his neck, he has thus far spent his retirement years trying to distance himself from Bush's disastrous economic policies.

These kids look like the older students at my school who smoke the funny-smelling cigarettes behind the gym.

THE STORY OF BANKS

COMMERCIAL BANK

FEDERAL RESERVE BANK

SAVINGS AND LOAN ASSOCIATION

MUTUAL SAVINGS BANK

CREDIT UNION

FEDERAL RESERVE BANK OF NEW YORK

[**FUN FACT**]

According to former paramour Barbara Walters, Greenspan is "a very nice dancer."

May 8, 1999

Dear Mr. Rukeyser,

This is a project for school. We are doing a unit on money and for extra credit we can write a letter asking a question. My question is what is the fastest easiest way to save up enough money for a speedboat? My dad said You were real smart about money. I make $10.00 a week allowance and I make $20.00 a month helping my brother deliver newspapers. Could You allso send me a picture?

Thanks,
Billy

Louis Rukeyser

This always impeccably attired and groomed broadcaster was a more genteel forerunner to today's generation of money news loudmouths like CNBC's Jim Cramer (who favors the sweaty, rolled-up sleeves "look"). Rukeyser, who died in 2006 at the age of seventy-three, was a very influential financial journalist with his own show, *Wall Street Week,* which ran on PBS for more than thirty years.

Is that word bullish or the naughty phrase my dad always uses when paying his speeding tickets?

For Billy Gearhart —
with the
bullish best
wishes of
Louis Rukeyser

GRAND HÔTEL
STOCKHOLM – SWEDEN

For Mr. Riggott's Economics Class,

Nobel Week,

Robert C. Merton

December 1997

Postal adress
P.O. Box 16424
S-103 27 STOCKHOLM

Street address
S. Blasie-
holmshamnen 8

Telephone
08-679 35 00

Telegram
Grand
Stockholm

Telefax
08-611 86 86

Telex
19500
Grand S

A member of
The Leading Hotels of the World

STEIGENBERGER
H·O·T·E·L·S

Robert C. Merton

The Nobel Prize–winning economist and author is a professor at the Harvard Business School. In the years since receiving Mr. Merton's well-reasoned, conservative advice, Billy has been disappointed to learn that his money guru has had some very risky associations. Specifically, Merton was on the board of directors of Long-Term Capital Management, a hedge fund that lost over $4 billion in 1998 and had to be bailed out under the supervision of the Federal Reserve before closing in 2000. The Nobel laureate was also the chief science officer for the financial advisory firm Trinsum Group, which went bankrupt in 2009 with millions in liabilities. Well, he'll always have Stockholm!

ROBERT C. MERTON
John and Natty McArthur University Professor

MORGAN HALL 397
BOSTON, MASSACHUSETTS 02163
617-495-6678
FAX: 617-495-8863
rmerton@hbs.edu

March 29, 1999

Dear Billy,

Thank you for your letter. Unfortunately, I cannot answer your question for two reasons: 1) I don't know how much a speed boat costs and 2) I don't know the _fastest_ way to make money. I can tell you that depending on the rate of return you can earn, how to figure out how long it would take you. From your letter, you are earning about $65 per month from allowance and helping your brother. At 6 percent interest, if you save all your money, then in 10 years you will have $10,650. The answer to your question in general is called the future-value-of-an-annuity problem. Good luck.

Best wishes,

Robert C. Merton

P.S. Picture and a little story of my life is in the enclosed reprint. See Page 12

April 13, 1999

Dear Milken,

I am writing to you for extra credit in my economics unit in Mr. Riggott's class. I was told you know a lot about economics, I would like to ask what is the fastest easiest way to save enough money for a speedboat? I earn $10.00 a week allowance and $20.00 a month helping my brother deliver the newspaper. If you can please send me a signed picture too.

Thanks,
Billy

Michael Milken

This formerly bewigged Wall Street junk-bond king lost his toupee (and hundreds of millions of dollars in fines) when he entered a federal prison in 1991 after plea bargaining to six counts of securities and reporting felonies. With the aid of attorney Alan Dershowitz, Milken got his ten-year sentence reduced, and he was back on the streets by 1993 looking to rehab his image. Despite all his humanitarian efforts and incessant lobbying since leaving the slammer, the billionaire felon has not yet earned the presidential pardon that he so desperately craves.

Here are some new secret messages for you to decode.

Mike's Math Club
Secret Coded Letter Values

0 = '	9 = N	18 = D
1 = F	10 = I	19 = B
2 = M	11 = L	20 = P
3 = H	12 = R	21 = W
4 = G	13 = X	22 = T
5 = O	14 = C	23 = Q
6 = A	15 = J	24 = Z
7 = S	16 = Y	25 = U
8 = E	17 = K	26 = V

A) 2, 6, 22, 3 - 14, 6, 9 - 19, 8 - 2, 6, 4, 10, 14 - 6, 9, 18 -

2, 6, 4, 10, 14 - 14, 6, 9 - 2, 6, 17, 8 - 16, 5, 25 - 6 - 21, 10, 24!

B) 12, 10, 18, 8 - 22, 3, 8 - 6, 11, 4, 8, 19, 12, 6 - 22, 12, 6, 10, 9 -

21, 10, 22, 3 - 4, 5, 11, 18, 8, 9, 22, 6, 10, 11.

C) 1, 10, 26, 8 - 22, 10, 2, 8, 7 - 1, 10, 26, 8 - 10, 7 -

22, 21, 8, 9, 22, 16 - 22, 21, 5.   6, 20, 12, 10, 11 - 1, 5, 5, 11, 7!

APRIL 14, 1999

Dear Billy,

I received your letter to Mr. Milken and I sent it to his office. I know he'll be delighted to receive it and he'll try to answer you soon. He's very busy and he travels alot, so I don't know how long it might take.

Meanwhile here are a few things for you from Mike's Math Club. I hope you enjoy them.

Good luck in all your classes. You're a smart boy and I know you'll have your boat someday.

Sincerely,

Cammie Cohen

CAMMIE COHEN

Perhaps Mr. Milken would have gotten his pardon if he had written back to Little Billy like his assistant said he would.

September 7, 1999

Dear Mr. Hubbell,

This is a project for my school. We are doing a unit on money and our teacher Mr. Riggott said we could write people for extra credit. My Dad said you were smart and that I should write to you. My question is what is the fastest way to save up for a speedboat? I have an allowance and a paper route. My Dad helped me find your address.

Thanks,
Billy

Webb Hubbell

This vaguely remembered Whitewater figure with a weight problem spent eighteen months in federal prison on mail fraud and tax evasion convictions. Hubbell, an Arkansas crony of the Clintons, swindled more than $390,000 while he was a partner at the Rose Law Firm, the same Little Rock outfit that employed the future first lady of the United States and right-wing conspiracy perennial, Vince Foster. In 1994 Hubbell's creative billing practices from Rose caught up with him in Washington, where he was by then in the number three post at the Justice Department. The 320-pound associate attorney general resigned in disgrace and soon found himself in a minimum-security facility, where he was awarded the nickname of "The Big Easy" for his relaxed manner and expansive waistline. Hubbell served his time, wrote the obligatory confessional memoir, and eventually became an executive with an insurance company that brokers coverage for pot smokers.

October 10, 1999

Billy Geerhart

Dear Billy:

Thank you for your letter. It took a long time for it to reach me so I hope I am not writing back to late for your class project. Your project is very interesting as well as your desire to save up enough money for a speedboat. Every dream is worth striving for so good luck.

Here are a few ideas:

1. Get some of your friends who also want a speedboat to save there money with you. Boats are owned by friends all the time, and riding in a boat with friends is a lot more fun than being alone.

2. Maybe, you could ask your family to match whatever you are able to save so your savings will grow much faster.

3. When you get enough money talk to an investment advisor about the best way to grow your money.

4. Write speedboat manufacturers about your dream telling them why you want to save your money to buy a boat. You never know what they may be able to help you accomplish.

You never know what you can accomplish if you are persistent, and keep focusing on your goal. Good luck!

Sincerely,

Webb Hubbell

[**FUN FACT**]

Hubbell dropped one hundred pounds in jail.

Be

I'm so glad that

Through
special abo
to each oth
can be devel
Christ. A le
helps me as a

I have lo
le write to me
hen I write bac
his continues to
a blessing to
at your needs wi
d.

Billy, I guess
Lord to make me a
e to write me any
ough. I will keep
e and needs in my ha
a vow that God has he
ministry.

No power of satan...
roying spirit...will o
Spirit lives in the he
uman weaknesses exist,
lack. "If God be for
ns 8:31). This includes

want to be your Partner

S. I' be sending my little
ed Do   gs." May Goc

10.

[Fun with Tippy]

January 6, 1999

Dear Rev. Bakker,

I think my Dog Tippy's posesed by a Demon or the Ghost of my Grampa Jim. Would You write me back about what I should do? my friend Eddie said I should shoot Tippy. I will wait until I hear from You.

Thanks,
Billy

→

Jim Bakker

The controversial televangelist, along with his weepy, mascara-loving wife, Tammy Faye, became tabloid sensations in the late 1980s when their Christian TV and theme-park empire collapsed amid a sex and finance scandal. Bakker, who admitted to an indiscretion with a New Jersey church secretary named Jessica Hahn, served nearly five years in prison for mail and wire fraud and conspiracy. Tammy Faye divorced the disgraced pastor while he was incarcerated so that she could marry their former building contractor. Bakker has since returned to the Christian airwaves in Branson, Missouri, with *The Jim Bakker Show*, cohosted by his new wife, Lori. Tammy Faye died of cancer in 2007.

> . . . God hath not given us the spirit of fear, but of power, and of love, and of a sound mind.
>
> (II Timothy 1:7)

Dear Billy,

Just read your letter to Rev. Bakker.

In our pray time we were praying for you.

We feel you should not shoot Tippy.

We hope all is better and Tippy is back to normal.

God Bless you.

Your friend,

Leanne

Dear Billy,

Just read your letter to Rev. Bakker.

In our pray time we were praying for you.

We feel you should not shoot Tippy—

We hope all is better and Tippy is back to normal.

God Bless you.

your friend,

Leanne

[FUN FACT]

One of Bakker's prison cellmates was the perennial presidential candidate and conspiracy theorist Lyndon LaRouche.

ORAL ROBERTS

January 26, 1999

Mr. Billy Geerhart

Little Billy has read Oral's letter ten times and still can't figure out whether to shoot the dog. Maybe it is in Bible code.

Dear Billy,

I'm so glad that you contacted this ministry.

Through the years I've discovered there's something very special about two people coming into a partnership by writing to each other. I've seen so often that a closer relationship can be developed -- in my situation, a deeper relationship in Christ. A letter, when it reflects true feelings and needs, helps me as a minister of the Gospel to serve you better.

I have long had a ministry of answering the letters people write to me. I always pray over what is shared with me, then I write back with something good from God's Holy Word. This continues to be a blessing to many people and I hope it is a blessing to you...especially to know that I have prayed that your needs will be met through the power and glory of God.

Billy, I guess what I am trying to say is, I really want the Lord to make me a blessing to your life. Please feel free to write me any time and let me know what you are going through. I will keep it confidential. Then I will hold your name and needs in my hands and pray and write you back. This is a vow that God has helped me keep for these many years of this ministry.

No power of satan...including witchcraft, voodoo or a destroying spirit...will overcome God or His people. The Holy Spirit lives in the hearts of God's people, and while our human weaknesses exist, God's strengths make up for our human lack. "If God be for us, who can be against us?" (Romans 8:31). This includes you!

I want to be your Partner.

Your Partner for miracles,

Oral Roberts

P.S. I'll be sending my little pamphlet, "If You Need To Be Healed Do These Things." May God bless it to you.

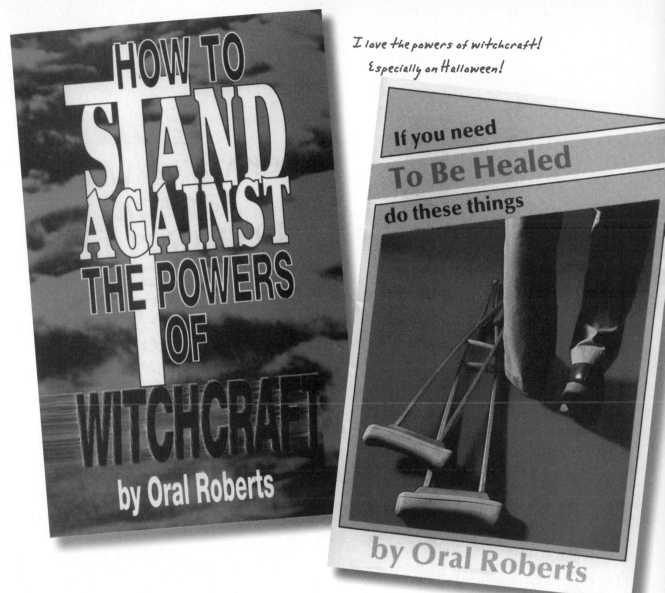

I love the powers of witchcraft!
Especially on Halloween!

Oral Roberts

This Oklahoma-born faith healer, televangelist, and Christian university founder once famously cited his vision of a 900-foot Jesus as the inspiration for his construction of a hospital. In 1987 Roberts used his own mortality as a fund-raising gimmick when he told his television audience that God would "call him home" if his ministry didn't receive $8 million in donations by the end of March of that year. The self-ransom exceeded all expectations with a reported $9.1 million pouring into the coffers by the deadline. Roberts, now in his nineties and semiretired, is still awaiting the call.

May 6, 1999

Dear Mr. Ettinger,

My dog Tippy died yesterday. My friend Eddie and me put Tippy in the bottom of my Dad's bait and meat freezer in the garage. Could you tell me how to bring Tippy back? or could you help? How much do you charge? Eddie says he heard about you on the innernet. Please write me back soon. If this helps I think Tippy died because of her heart.

Thank You, Billy

Cryonics Institute

The founder and no doubt future client of the Michigan-based organization that freezes people after they die is the nonagenarian Robert C. W. Ettinger, a man known as "the father of cryonics" because of his influential 1962 book *The Prospect of Immortality*. In 1977 none other than Ettinger's own mother was the Cryonics Institute's first "patient." Since that historic maternal refrigeration, Ettinger has also put his first and second wives on ice. As of 2009, the Institute had ninety-three humans and sixty pets stored in liquid nitrogen awaiting future reanimation . . . and uncomfortable family reunions.

CRYONICS INSTITUTE
24355 Sorrentino Court
Clinton Township MI 48035
Phone (810) 791-5961, Phone/Fax (810) 792-7062
E-Mail Cryonics@Cryonics.org
Web Site <http://www.cryonics.org>

R.C.W. Ettinger
3326 N. 81 St.
Scottsdale AZ 85251
Phone (602) 941-5591, Fax (602) 947-7759, email ettinger@aol.com

May 10, 1999

Billy Geerhart

Dear Billy--

When you have read this, please show it to your parents.

First of all, I know how distressing it is to lose a friend, whether human or not. But you will almost certainly lose more friends in the course of your life, and you need to be able to deal with it. Sometimes it makes sense to fight, but sometimes it doesn't. You are smart and brave, but you can't always win.

Tippy was frozen by crude means, without cryoprotectant solution. Even if she had been frozen under the best conditions, most scientists would rate her chance of revival--ever--as near zero. We are much more optimistic than most scientists, but the possibility of revival must be balanced against the cost.

It will not help to keep her in the freezer. At your freezer temperature, deterioration is relatively rapid, even though her external appearance will not change much. Liquid nitrogen storage is much more expensive; we charge $6,000 for a cat or any animal the size of a cat, plus a $1,250 membership fee for the owner. Unless your parents are so wealthy that the expense is unimportant, and unless they are willing, you must accept the loss and get on with your life. At least you know that Tippy isn't suffering--she is just gone, and you can take some comfort in your knowledge that you shared some happy times.

When you are able, I hope you and your parents will study the material on our web site and, when you are ready, make arrangements for yourselves. I hope to meet you one day.

Best wishes--

Ettinger

Six thousand dollars to freeze a cat?!
Eddie says he could do that for free.

May 6, 1999

Dear Mr. Chamberlain,

My dog Tippy died yesterday. My friend Eddie and me put Tippy in the bottom of my Dad's meat freezer in the garage. Could you tell me how to bring Tippy back or could you help? How much do you charge? Eddie heard about you on the innernet. Please write back soon! If this helps I think Tippy died of a heart attack.

Thanks,
Billy

Alcor Life Extension Foundation

The Scottsdale, Arizona–based cryonics organization is best known for its star "patient," Boston Red Sox legend Ted Williams, who was "cryopreserved" at their facility after his death on July 5, 2002. At Alcor, the Hall of Famer's head was decapitated for "neuropreservation," and, perhaps anticipating another season at Fenway in the distant future, the power hitter's body is also being preserved in a tank of liquid nitrogen. In 2005 Williams's son, John Henry Williams, who had died of leukemia, joined his father in suspended animation at the facility (make up your own *Field of Dreams* joke). As of 2009, Alcor had eighty-five cryopreserved humans and an undisclosed number of pets.

Alcor LIFE EXTENSION FOUNDATION

May 11, 1999

Billy Geerhart

Little Billy likes the guy turning into the dragon after his long ice nap.

Dear Billy:

I was very sorry to hear about the loss of your dog, Tippy. Having lost many pets myself, I know how sad you must feel.

Unfortunately, the Alcor Foundation can only provide storage for human cryonics patients. I am afraid there is nothing we can do for your pet.

However, you might contact a company called "Canine Cryobank." Although I do not know exactly how much they charge (around $400, I believe), I believe they will freeze and store a tissue sample containing your pet's DNA for possible future cloning. You can contact them at:

Canine Cryobank
120 N. Pacific A5
San Marcos, CA 92069
Telephone: 760.591.9909
Fax: 760.591.9939
email: info@caninecryobank.com
web site: http://www.caninecryobank.com

Again, I am very sorry that we cannot help you.

Respectfully,

Brian Shock
Membership Manager

[**FUN FACT**]

The foundation does not freeze animals unless their owners are members because, as their website states, "It makes no sense to send a pet into the future if the owner will not be there for them."

May 14, 1999

Dear People,

About a week ago my dog Tippy died. We (my friend Eddie and me) put Tippy in the bottom of my Dad's meat freezer. A guy at a company called ALcor said you could clone Tippy. How much would this cost? Would Tippy come back to life as a puppy? Would she still be house broke? Please write back as soon as you can!

Thank You,
BILLY

Canine Cryobank

While Canine Cryobank, a DNA preservation and pet-breeding company founded in Los Angeles in 1981, has not yet cloned any dogs, there have been major advances in the field since Billy's letter. Indeed, the first commercial canine cloning took place in South Korea in 2008 by a company called RNL Bio. An American woman named Joyce Bernann McKinney had five puppies cloned from her late pit bull, Booger, at a reported cost of $50,000. There may be hope for Tippy after all!

CANINE CRYOBANK, INC. SINCE 1981

Harvesting Cells for Future Pet Clones

In 17 years, Canine Cryobank's artificial insemination and breeding assistance services added 16,000 patients to the veterinary industry :, 11,000 locally in San Diego, Riverside, Orange Counties.
Our cell storage and future pet clones offer remarkable possibilities for the veterinary medicine industry's future......

Carol Scott Bardwick
Founder/President

CANINE CRYOBANK, INC.
SINCE 1981

Dear Billy,

I am sorry to hear about Tippy.

It is possible that some cells from Tippy could be grown in culture but only slightly possible , since Tippy was put into the freezer which lessens the chances of cells surviving....

Advances in cloning are rapid. If you keep some of Tippy's fur, MAYBE, someday, someone will discover how to take the DNA out of the fur and start cell culture with Tippy's DNA. In your lifetime, many incredible things will be possible.

A very good source of information on cloning for you and your friends is "Science Explained" by Dr. Jamie Love, http://www. synapse.ndirect.co.uk/science/clone.html

To answer your questions: Tippy would come back as a pup and you would have to housebreak her.

Sincerely,

Carol Scott Bardwick

Carol Scott Bardwick

120 N. PACIFIC A-5
SAN MARCOS, CA 92069
760 591 9909 FAX 5919939

E-MAIL K9CRYO@PACBELL.NET
CANINECRYOBANK.COM

[FUN FACT]

The extensive publicity that accompanied the bioengineering feat of the "Booger Cloning" exposed Joyce Bernann McKinney's bizarre criminal history as a fugitive from the United Kingdom. In 1977 the wacky pet lover and former beauty queen abducted a Mormon missionary she was obsessed with and attempted to make him her sex slave. She escaped England while on bail by pretending to be a member of a mime troupe.

COULD THERE EVER BE ANOTHER??....

MOST TITLED MALAMUTE IN HISTORY
MULTIPLE BEST IN SHOW BEST IN SPECIALTY SHOW
(AMERICAN/MEXICAN/CANADIAN/EUROPEAN/BERMUDA/
INTERNATIONAL/ WORLD/CAC/CACIB/CH/FCM
CH. CHINOME'S ARCTIC INVADER
CD PC PCX TT CGC IWPA WPD WPD WTD WLD WWPD IWPAX
WPDX WPDX WTDX WLDX WWPDX

FROZEN CELLS FOR CLONING

CANINE CRYOBANK, INC.
CAROL BARDWICK, EXECUTIVE PROP.

11

To Billy Gearhart,

If Connie agrees, it would be a good agreement. Best wishes.

Warren Christopher

3-19-99

[Treehouse Diplomacy]

James A. Baker III

This statesman, lawyer, and Bush family fixer first got into politics managing George H. W. Bush's losing 1970 Texas Senate race. Baker later served as President Ronald Reagan's chief of staff and treasury secretary and Bush Sr.'s secretary of state during the Persian Gulf War. In 2000 he acted as George W. Bush's chief legal adviser during the Florida recount and successfully outmaneuvered his counterpart on Vice President Al Gore's team, former Secretary of State Warren Christopher. Baker would attempt to help Junior again three years later when he publicly advocated for more diplomatic efforts prior to the Iraq War. When that advice went famously unheeded, it left many to wonder whether Baker regretted ever getting on that plane to Florida.

March 23, 1999

Dear Mr. Baker,
This is a project for my school. our teacher Mr. Riggott said we could get extra credit if we wrote to a statesman. I wanted to ask you to look at this treaty I want to make with my sister. If you think it is a good treaty I will make it law. I would also really like a picture signed to me. my teacher helped me find your address.
Thank You,
Billy Geerhart

TREATY
CONNIE GEERHART. WILL STAY OUT OF BILLY GEERHART'S TREEHOUSE AND BILLY GEERHART WILL STOP THROWING CONNIE GEERHART'S DOLLS OUT the WINDOW.
THIS TREATY LASTS ONE YEAR

BILLY GEERHART   CONNIE GEERHART
DATE

JAMES A. BAKER, III

ONE SHELL PLAZA
910 LOUISIANA
HOUSTON, TEXAS 77002-4995

April 7, 1999

Dear Billy:

Thank you for writing to me to ask for my advice on your treaty. This is one of the most unique treaties I have ever reviewed.

You did not say in your letter how old you and Connie are, but I suggest that you may want to extend the treaty so that it covers a two year period. Except for that one change, I think your treaty is excellent.

Good luck with your school project,

Sincerely,

Jim Baker

James A. Baker, II

Mr. Billy Geerhart

James Baker puts the "power" in "power broker"! No wonder Warren Christopher looks so depressed.

To Billy Geerhart with very best wishes Jim Baker

To Billy Gearhart,

if Connie agrees, it would be
a good agreement. Best wishes.

Warren Christopher

3-19-99

Warren Christopher

President Bill Clinton's Bela Lugosi–esque first-term secretary of state is currently a power lawyer in Los Angeles. When Christopher's perfunctory 1999 diplomatic advice to Billy is compared to the more polished response of fellow statesman James A. Baker III, it becomes easier to see how the latter outmaneuvered the former in the Florida recount showdown a year later.

Christopher's losing performance in that battle of wills apparently still rankles—in 2008 he complained to the *New York Times* about his depiction as a weak strategist in the HBO dramatization *Recount*. The film starred Tom Wilkinson as a cocksure, calculating Baker and John Hurt as a tentative, ineffectual Christopher. In the same *Times* article Christopher's former adversary backed him up, kind of, with this delightful bit of hedging: ". . . I know he was not as wimpish as it makes him appear."

OFFICE OF
HENRY A. KISSINGER

May 26, 1999

Dear Billy:

Dr. Kissinger was traveling out of town
when your letter arrived. But he asked me
to tell you that he approves of your treaty
and agrees that you should make it law.

Good luck with your treehouse--and your
sister!

Sincerely,

Theresa L. Cimino

Theresa L. Cimino
Assistant to Dr. Kissinger

Master Billy Geerhart

To. Billy Geerhart
Every good wish

TWENTY-SIXTH FLOOR · 350 PARK AVENUE · NEW YORK, NEW YORK 10022 · (212) 759-7919

[FUN FACT]

During the 1973 Yom Kippur War, Kissinger helped a "loaded" Richard Nixon dodge a telephone call from the British prime minister.

Henry Kissinger

This German-born Nobel Peace Prize–winning überstatesman was on the faculty of Harvard University when President Richard Nixon recruited him to be his national security adviser and later his secretary of state. During his controversial tenure in government, Kissinger reveled in his celebrity and referred to power as "the ultimate aphrodisiac"—a maxim that falls apart when applied to Nixon. In between dates with Jill St. John and other stars, the randy diplomat helped his president cynically manipulate foreign policy for short-term political advantage. Kissinger is best known for his work in the opening of relations with China, negotiating the end of the Vietnam War, and praying with a drunken Nixon as his presidency imploded. In recent years the former secretary of state and alleged war criminal advised the Bush administration to stay the course in Iraq.

June 15, 1999 ★ Billy Geerhart

Dear Mr. MacNamara,

This is a project for my school.
We can write to a historical figure.
and ask a question.

My Dad said You were a great
military thinker. I want to ask You
about plans I have for my treehouse
fort. To keep my enemies out I
want to dig a mote and fill it
with water. What do you think
of this idea? Do You think it will
work? please write back!

7/8/99
It will work if You dig it deep   Thank You,
enough, and r. flour covercds
can't swim!   Billy
Best wishes, Robert S. McNamara

7/8/00
It will work if you dig it deep
enough; and your enemies
can't swim!
Best Wishes,
Robert S. McNamara

Robert S. McNamara

This secretary of defense under Presidents John F. Kennedy and Lyndon B. Johnson was one of the key architects of the Vietnam War and became inextricably linked in history to the conflict. Before serving in government, McNamara was president of the Ford Motor Company, where, earlier in his career, he had tried unsuccessfully to prevent the automotive marketing disaster known as the Edsel. Vietnam would mark the second debacle the former so-called Whiz Kid failed to stop. Most people have forgiven him for the Edsel. Years after McNamara resigned as secretary of defense to run the World Bank, an artist angry over the war recognized him on a ferry and tried to throw him overboard. McNamara passed away in 2009 at the age of ninety-three.

April 21, 2004

Dear Mr. Rumsfeld,

My friend Eddie and I are going to invade Jimmie Halprin's treehouse because he's a bully. Do you think we should do this at night? Eddie says your real smart. Please allso sign my Enduring Freedom card. You are a great American!

Thanks!

Billy

Donald Rumsfeld

The former Illinois congressman was a two-time secretary of defense under Presidents Gerald Ford and George W. Bush. Rumsfeld is best known for his spirited enablement of neocon fantasy projects like the preemptive war in Iraq and his virtuoso press-conference performances defending same. In 2003 the secretary brushed aside concern over widespread looting after the fall of Baghdad with the phrase "stuff happens." When challenged by a soldier about inadequate body and vehicle armor, Rumsfeld came up with this gem: "You go to war with the army you have, not the army you might want . . ." Reportedly Rumsfeld kept his born-again commander-in-chief pumped about the Iraq invasion by using Christian-themed cover sheets on daily intelligence briefings. Bush finally fired his Strangelovian defense secretary in 2006 and replaced him with the refreshingly bland Robert Gates.

THE SECRETARY OF DEFENSE
WASHINGTON

MAY 10 2004

Reading between the lines, Little Billy took Rummy's advice and attacked Jimmy's tree house. It turned into a total quagmire.

Master Billy Geerhart

Dear Billy,

Your letter arrived. I am afraid I don't know what to advise with respect to your plans, but I was delighted to sign your Enduring Freedom card.

Thanks for your support!

Warm regards,

Sincerely,

[signature]

Defere Secretary Rumsfeld Makes A Point

★ Defense Secretary Rumsfeld Makes A Point ★

Secretary of Defense Donald Rumsfeld is hardly a stranger to the office, having served in that same capacity, from 1975-1977, during the Ford administration. Indeed, he was then the youngest Defense Secretary in the country's history. Within days of the tragedy, Rumsfeld stated that the Bush administration was moving carefully to launch a sustained offensive against not only the terrorists responsible for the attacks, but also the nations that support them. He explained that the fight against terrorism would require a broad effort and that "a lot of it will be special operations," referring to the military's elite forces, such as Army Green Berets and Navy SEALs.

THE NATION'S LEADERS

34

can scare my sister and protect
my treehouse. It should
his

Bot

sist

HO

12.

[Free with
Purchase]

Dear Nesquik Bunny,
My mom who used to be a hippy
says I can't drink your shake
anymore because your a
comercial tool whatever that
means, She allso said your shake
causes cancer, please write her
and tell her she's wrong. Please
send some Nesquik too!

Thanks,
Billy

The NESQUIK Bunny

The manic shake-loving Nestlé corporate
spokescharacter was born in 1973 as "Quiky" and has
bonded with generations of sugar-craving children.

February 22, 2002

Little Billy really admires Mr. Bunny for being the only fictional character brave enough to respond directly.

Mr. Billy Geerhart

Dear Mr. Geerhart,

Thank you for taking the time to contact me about NESTLÉ NESQUIK. I appreciate your letter and am glad you have been so loyal to my NESQUIK. I do hope you like the Fun Facts and Activity Book I am sending to you. I sent them along just for you.

Here at the NESQUIK factory I am hard at work making the chocolate milk for my loyal fans, such as you, Billy. Thank you so much for writing to me and please enjoy these coupons for some NESQUIK. And remember, "You can't drink it slow if it's Quik!"

Sincerely,

The NesQuik Bunny

Ref: 7530464
enclosure

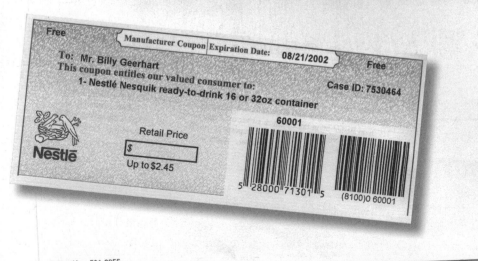

© Nestlé   501-0055

Dear Mr. Leprachaun,
My mother who used to be a hippy
says I can't eat your cereal
because your a comercial fool, I don't
know what this means. She allso
said your cereal causes cancer,
could you write my mother back and
tell her she's wrong? Please send
me some cereal too!

Thanks,
Billy

The Lucky Charms Leprechaun

The sprightly yet paranoid ("They're always after me Lucky Charms!") cereal mascot was created in 1963 as a tie-in to the original ad-agency-concocted-marketing-gimmick charm bracelets. But it was the peculiar Irish cartoon character that caught the public's fancy and has stuck around for nearly half a century. With his intriguing catchphrase "They're magically delicious" and poorly animated commercial adventures, Sir Charms and his sugary product appeal to stoners and kids alike.

General Mills Consumer Services

P.O. Box 1113, Minneapolis, MN 55440

March 26, 2002

Mr. Billy Geerhart

Dear Mr. Geerhart:

Thank you for contacting General Mills. We are sorry you were disappointed with our advertising for Lucky Charms. Our intent is to encourage both potential and existing customers to use our products. Your opinions are important to us and will be carefully reviewed with our marketing and advertising staff.

We appreciate your interest and hope you continue to enjoy our products.

Sincerely,

Carol Brown

Carol Brown

Manufacturer coupon • Expires 03/31/2003

General Mills

Mr. Geerhart

This will authorize your retailer to give you 50¢ OFF

Any General Mills Food Product

(Excludes twin or triple pack cereals, Lloyd's, Colombo, Yoplait, Pillsbury, Green Giant, Progresso, Totino's, Jeno's or Old El Paso products).

One coupon per purchase. Consumer must pay any sales tax.
Void where prohibited, licensed or regulated.
THIS DOCUMENT IS PRINTED ON WHITE PAPER WITH A
PATTERNED BACKGROUND AND HAS A PRE-PRINTED BACK.

A1449/YCB/2002/03/26-0005

5 16000 00050 1 (8100)0 10000

General Offices at Number One General Mills Boulevard

Dear Tony,
My mother who used to be a hippy says I can't eat your cereal because your a comercial tool whatever that means. She allso said your cereal causes cancer. Could you write her and tell her she's wrong? Please send some cereal!
Thanks,
Billy

Tony the Tiger

Kellogg's alpha spokescharacter Tony the Tiger was created in 1951 by the Leo Burnett advertising agency, and his signature phrase "They're Grrrreat!" was growled for more than fifty years by voice-over star Thurl Ravenscroft. As the years went by, Tony had a family (Tony, Jr., had a brief failed spin-off cereal) and became more fit as the name of the product changed from Kellogg's Frosted *Sugar* Flakes to the healthier-sounding Kellogg's Frosted Flakes.

Kellogg's

March 14, 2002

Mr Billy Geerhart

Dear Mr Geerhart:

Thank you for contacting Kellogg Company. We appreciate your interest.

We certainly understand the importance of a good diet and the key role our products play in providing our consumers with healthy and nutritious food options at breakfast, or anytime during the day.

We remain committed to providing our consumers with cereal, convenience food and snacking options that not only offer a delicious, low-fat alternative, but also provide important vitamins and minerals needed for good physical and mental development. Our cereal brands offer all of these benefits at a very affordable price. You can still have a 1.5 ounce serving of cereal with milk for less than 30 cents, making ready-to-eat cereals an excellent value for the real health benefits they provide.

We hope we may count you among our valued family of Kellogg consumers in the years ahead as we continue to offer you delicious and nutritious products at a price you can afford.

Sincerely,

Jeanette Roebuck

Jeanette J. Roebuck
Consumer Specialist
Consumer Affairs Department

JJR/jji

4845668A

*Spoiler alert: Ms. Roebuck
also moonlights as an
assistant to E.L. Fudge.*

Kellogg Company / Porter Street Office Complex
235 Porter Street / Battle Creek, Michigan 49014

Dear Mr. Fudge,
My mother who used to be a hippy said I can't eat your fudge because your a comercial tool whatever that means, she allso said your fudge causes cancer. Could you please write my mom and tell her she's wrong? Please send some fudge too.

Thanks,
Billy

E.L. Fudge

There's not much of a backstory here except that the initials of the Keebler elf-shaped cookie product stand for "Everybody Loves" (fudge). The ad-agency elves punched out early on this one.

Keebler Company

P.O. Box CAMB

Battle Creek, MI 49016-1986

877.453.5837

March 14, 2002

Ms. Roebuck must be so busy with her two jobs working for Mr. Tiger and Mr. Fudge that she doesn't seem to notice when kids mention cancer in their letters.

Mr Billy Geerhart

Dear Mr Geerhart:

Thank you for taking the time to contact us.

It is our goal to consistently provide you with high quality products. Every effort is made to produce top quality products.

We appreciate your giving us the opportunity to respond to you. Please accept the enclosed coupon with our compliments.

Sincerely,

Jeanette Roebuck

Jeanette J. Roebuck
Consumer Specialist
Consumer Affairs Department

THANK YOU!

Thank you for contacting Keebler Company. We sincerely appreciate your comments and have forwarded them to the appropriate people. Please accept the attached coupon. We hope you will be pleased with your Keebler® selection the next time you shop.

KEEBLER COMPANY
CONSUMER AFFAIRS DEPARTMENT
P.O. BOX CAMB
BATTLE CREEK, MICHIGAN 49016-1986

Nº 011215

MANUFACTURER'S COUPON · NOT TO BE DOUBLED | EXPIRES 12/31/03

THIS COUPON IS GOOD FOR ONE

FREE* KEEBLER® PRODUCT *Up to $3.39

ERNIE BUCKS

GROCER-PLEASE FILL IN PRODUCT PRICE ABOVE (NOT TO EXCEED $3.39) FOR REDEMPTION

CONSUMER: Limit one coupon per purchase of product indicated. Void where taxed, restricted or prohibited. Consumer must pay sales tax. DEALER: We will reimburse you face value of this coupon (not to exceed $3.39) plus $.08 handling if in accordance with Keebler coupon redemption terms. Copies available upon request. Mail properly redeemed coupons to: Keebler Company, CMS Department 30100, 1 Fawcett Drive, Del Rio, TX 78840. Cash value 1/20 of $.01. © 2002 Keebler Company

5 30100 00001 1 (8100) 0 06463

CHEEZ-IT   Austin QUALITY   MURRAY   Famous Amos

E.L. FUDGE   185

Dear Sugar Bear,
my mother who used to be a hippy says I can't eat your cereal because your a comercial tool. I don't know what that means. my mom allso said your cereal causes cancer. could you write my mom and tell her she's wrong? Please send me some cereal.
Thanks!
Billy

Sugar Bear

Golden Crisp Cereal's refreshingly honest mascot appeals directly to the sugar-addicted child consumer with his repetitively encouraging theme song "Can't Get Enough of That Golden Crisp." The cereal and the character used to be even more blatant when the product was marketed as Sugar Crisp and Super Sugar Crisp.

Consumer Resource & Information Center

March 25, 2002

Mr. Billy Gerhart

Dear Mr. Gerhart:

Thank you for writing to us about the concerns your mother has about our Golden Crisp cereal.

If you could pass this information to your mother, we would like to explain why we believe our cereal is a wholesome, high quality cereal:

The list of ingredients on packaged foods often appear complex and quite technical. The names of the compounds in foods often have lengthy, technical names. For example, there are more than 80 compounds that occur naturally in milk, and these compounds have names that are also very technical-sounding. We understand why you, as a parent, might be concerned.

The point is not to be concerned about a food's safety based on the words listed on the ingredient line. All foods, whether processed or not, are made up of numerous compounds having highly technical names. All ingredients and additives used in our products are used consistently with the Food and Drug Administration's (FDA) regulations. Any ingredient or additive is used at the minimum amount to achieve the desired effect. Please be assured that we uphold the highest standards for safe food products for you and your family.

Billy, I'm sorry but we can't send you some cereal because we receive requests such as yours on a daily basis and it would be virtually impossible to say "yes" to the tremendous amount of requests we receive so we have to say "no" to all. We hope this information helps, and thanks again for writing to us.

Sincerely,

Diane Mazek

*This person sure likes the word **technical**.*

Diane Mazek/km
Executive Representative

10210861/12378693/DM/kcs

Kraft Foods • (800) 323-0768

KRAFT FOODS One Kraft Court Glenview, Illinois 60025 • (800) 323-0768
For Food & Family Ideas Visit Our Website at www.kraftanswers.com

13

[Grab Bag]

April 9, 2004

Dear Governer Swarchineger,
Today I was sent home early from
school for pinching Bonnie Youker's butt.
My friend Eddie said You do this
all the time and I should write
to You to You to get My teacher
MRS. Buchalt fired. Please
Write me back and send me a
Cool picture!

Thanks,
Billy

Arnold Schwarzenegger

The Austrian-born bodybuilder landed in America in 1968 and by sheer force of will became a terrible actor, a mediocre governor, and a superb groper. Schwarzenegger, who cites the soaring rhetoric of Richard Nixon for his decision to become a Republican, can be seen in the documentary *Pumping Iron* acting more like a Democrat. Indeed, had Nixon been president when the film was released in 1977, he might have had Arnold deported for smoking a joint on camera and comparing weightlifting to sex. In 1984 Schwarzenegger beat out O. J. Simpson for the title role in *The Terminator*, the movie that would propel him to action-hero stardom and a series of talent-stretching vehicles like *Predator*, *Commando*, and *Junior*.

OFFICE OF THE GOVERNOR

Gov. Arnold should have been recalled for ignoring Billy's demand to fire his teacher.

July 2, 2004

Billy Geerhart

Dear Billy,

Thank you for your letter requesting my photo. I have enclosed one for your collection, with my compliments.

Again, thank you for taking the time to write.

Sincerely,

Arnold Schwarzenegger

Enclosure

[**FUN FACT**]

Among the people Schwarzenegger defeated to become Governator in the 2003 California Recall Election were pornographer Larry Flynt, *Diff'rent Strokes* actor Gary Coleman, and adult-film star Mary Carey.

GOVERNOR ARNOLD SCHWARZENEGGER • SACRAMENTO, CALIFORNIA 95814 • (916) 445-2841

Dear Mr. Heston,
My Dad likes to keep his gun next to the remote control on the cofee table, IS this safe? Please send me a coloring book,

Thanks!
Billy

a GUNSAFE educational book

THE EAGLE PAK WAY

National Rifle Association

The nonprofit gun-ownership rights and advocacy organization was founded in 1871 and has approximately four million members. The group is known for its powerful lobby in Washington and for its frequently overheated and paranoid rhetoric. In 1995 former president George H. W. Bush terminated his lifetime membership in the organization after receiving a fund-raising letter that referred to federal law-enforcement agents as "jackbooted Government thugs." In addition to former NRA president Charlton Heston, notable members past and present include convicted Oklahoma City bomber Timothy McVeigh, former Alaska governor Sarah Palin, and rocker Ted Nugent.

EDDIE EAGLE® PROGRAM

July 26, 2000

Little Billy loves Mr. Heston's movies that have the apes on horseback with rifles.

Mr. Billy Geerhart

Dear Billy:

Thank you for your recent letter to NRA's president Mr. Charlton Heston. Mr. Heston has asked me to respond on his behalf.

First, the most important thing you need to know is if you find a gun: **STOP! Don't Touch. Leave the Area. Tell an Adult.** This is the message of The Eddie Eagle GunSafe® Program. The program's mascot, Eddie Eagle, teaches children this safety lesson so kids will not hurt themselves or anyone else. I've enclosed an Eddie Eagle workbook for you. I hope you enjoy it and remember its important message.

If you are concerned about your father's firearm, I am sure he would want you to ask him about it. I have also enclosed a *Parent's Guide to Gun Safety* brochure which you can give to your father. It discusses the NRA's basic rule of gun storage is to "store your gun so it is inaccessible to any unauthorized user." If your father is indeed leaving the gun where untrained people might get to it, then no, we would not consider that safe.

Thanks for writing.

Sincerely,

Heidi A. Cifelli

Heidi A. Cifelli
Program Manager

Enclosures

[FUN FACT]

The NRA's online gift shop has a selection of stylish "Conceal Carry" purses for the ladies.

National Rifle Association
11250 Waples Mill Road • Fairfax, VA 22030 • Phone (800) 231.0752 • Fax (703) 267.3993

May 8, 1999

Dear Mr. Rogers,

My Mommy and me watch your T.V. show all the time. My Mommy said she heard you were sick and needed a new kidny to keep living and being on T.V. I wanted to tell you I would like to give you one of my kidnies if that will help. Could you allso send me a picture when you write back? I hope you feel better!

Thanks!

Billy

Mister Rogers

This beloved sweater-wearing children's television personality and ordained Presbyterian minister hosted the long-running program *Mister Rogers' Neighborhood* on PBS until 2001. Fred Rogers's soothing and simple manner of speech and his guileless personality were frequently satirized, most notably in a *National Lampoon Radio Hour* bit in which Christopher Guest played "Mr. Roberts" interviewing a stoned bass musician voiced by Bill Murray. And Eddie Murphy moved the neighborhood to the ghetto for his recurring parody of the program on *Saturday Night Live*. The saintly Rogers died of stomach cancer in 2003.

Family Communications, Inc.
4802 Fifth Avenue
Pittsburgh, Pennsylvania 15213
412/687-2990

May, 1999

Billy Geerhart

Dear Billy,

What a caring person you are! It was very kind of you to write to me when your mother told you that I was sick and needed a new kidney. And it meant so much to me that you wanted to give me one of your kidneys.

Billy, I'm glad to tell you that I am not sick, and I don't need a new kidney. I wonder what your mother heard. Maybe it was about another person whose last name is Rogers. I'm happy to tell you that I am in good health. But I was very touched by your kindness.

It gives me such a good feeling to know you enjoy our Neighborhood visits. And it's wonderful to know you and your mother watch it together. I'm proud to have a television friend like you. And you are fortunate to have a mother who cares so much about you and about the things that are important to you.

Did you know about our 1-4-3 message? I've talked about that a few times on our television program. It stands for "I LOVE YOU" -- I (1 alphabet letter), LOVE (4 letters), YOU (3 letters). There's even a lighthouse in Nantucket that sends a light message of 1-4-3! When I looked at your address, I saw you have a 1-4-3 in it! Your letter certainly was a 1-4-3 message to me. Thank you for helping to make it a more beautiful day in this Neighborhood.

Lots of good wishes from all of us here in the Neighborhood. You are special -- just because you're you.

Your television friend,

Mister Rogers

Dear FEMA,
My family is very scared of atomic attack. Could you please tell me what a kid my age ←I'M 11 years old should have packed for a fallout shelter? My Dad said my dog wouldn't be allowed because of food. Do you think that's fair? Do you have any coloring books about shelters? Please write me back before the atomic war.

Thanks,
Billy

Federal Emergency Management Agency (FEMA)

The government's disaster-preparedness agency became synonymous with failure for its handling of the Hurricane Katrina response in 2005. Under the feckless leadership of President Bush's hack political appointee Michael "Heckuva Job Brownie" Brown, the agency proved to be stunningly ill equipped for the storm's devastation of New Orleans. In the years since Katrina, FEMA has also become known for its useless formaldehyde-scented emergency-housing trailers.

FEMA coloring books are cool, but couldn't they have at least included a letter telling my dad that it was OK to let the dog in the fallout shelter?

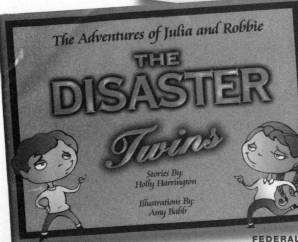

April 26, 2004

Dear Mr. Ridge,
This is a project for school. We're
supposed to write to the Goverment
and make a suggestion to make
America better. I think America
would be better if your Department
gave kids lunchboxes with the color
codes on them so kids know what
the colors mean. We're orange
now Right? Would You also sign my
Enduring Freedom Card?
Thanks,
Billy ⟹

Mr. Ridge was too busy changing the alert colors to sign his Enduring Freedom card.

U.S. Secretary Of Homeland Security Tom Ridge

Tom Ridge

The Vietnam veteran and moderate Republican governor of Pennsylvania was tapped by President George W. Bush to head the newly formed Office of Homeland Security (later Department of Homeland Security) shortly after the 9/11 attacks. The beefy Ridge will probably forever be remembered for his unveiling of the universally ridiculed color-coded Homeland Security Advisory System (aka the Terror Alert Chart) in 2002. The curious timing of the alert-level changes—and their apparent political benefit to the president—is another legacy the former DHS secretary carries (but tried to distance himself from, in his 2009 memoir *The Test of Our Times*). In the years since he left government, Ridge has joined various lucrative company boards including Home Depot, which experienced a surge in duct-tape sales during one particularly memorable Orange Alert in 2003.

July 2, 2000

Dear Mr. Goldin,
My little sister bugs me a lot and
my friend Eddie said NASA has a
time travel ship that maybe could
be used to send her back in time.
If this is true I'd like to send
her back to the time of the
Dinosores. How much would this
cost? Please write me
back!

Thank you,
Billy

NASA

The National Aeronautics and Space Administration was created in 1958 and well funded by
Congress to compete in the Cold War space race with the Soviet Union. Since the historic
manned moon landing of 1969, however, NASA has gradually lost the fascination of the public.
Today the space agency is known more for its obsessed, diaper-wearing, cross-country-driving
astronauts than it is for its shuttle missions.

National Aeronautics and
Space Administration

Headquarters
Washington, DC 20546-0001

Reply to Attn of: M-9

Mr. Billy Geerhart

SEP 2 0 2000

Dear Billy:

Thank you for your letter of July 2, 2000, regarding your question about NASA spacecraft.

NASA does not have a time travel ship. We do have the Space Shuttle, which carries astronauts into space for missions lasting up to two weeks at a time. We are currently building the International Space Station, a laboratory and home in space, which will house astronauts beginning this Fall. I have included some information about these NASA spacecraft for you information.

If you want to learn more about what we do at NASA, please see:
http://www.nasa.gov/kids.html
This site includes games and fun activities for you to enjoy.

Thank you for your interest in NASA's spacecraft. Please accept my best wishes in your future endeavors.

Sincerely,

Kirsten Williams

Kirsten Williams
Public Affairs Specialist
For Space Flight

[FUN FACT]

President Nixon's speechwriter William Safire had a contingency speech ready in the event the Apollo 11 astronauts were stranded on the moon.

✸ Join the y.c.l.

Via Snail-Mail

Please print this page, fill out the form below and then mail it when you are done. Please include $1 for your initiation fee and $1 for your first year of dues. Within 2-3 weeks, you will receive in the mail: 1 free issue of the YCL magazine Dynamic, a YCL pin, a new members packet.

Mail to:
YCL-USA
235 W. 23rd Street
New York, NY 10011

Little Billy was so glad that his revolutionary brothers and sisters broke the narrow rules of the Party and allowed him early membership. He actually just wanted the card and cool button.

MEMBERSHIP FORM
Young Communist League, USA
Contact Information

First [Billy] Last [Geerhart]

Mailing Address (and Apt. #) [ ]

City [ ] State [ ] Zip [ ]

Home phone [Unlisted] Work phone [ ] → *I don't work, but I have a paper route*

e-mail [My Dad's]

Please **do not** contact me by ☐ home phone ☐ home mail ☐ e-mail

Birthdate [Aug. 26, 1989] Gender [Boy] Racial/National Origin [American]

[Yes] I want to build a YCL club in my school, workplace, or neighborhood.

Brief Personal Statement

The reason I want to join the YCL is... [because I want to learn about COMMUNISM and help my sister and my freid become Communist.]

Education (optional)

I am in school now, or have attended [ ]

My school's name, city, state is [schoolname, city, state] Los Feliz Elementary

L.A., Ca.

Work Info (optional)

http://www.yclusa.org/join/join_ana.html

The Young Communist League, USA

The YCL, an organization not to be confused with the capitalist superhero collective known as the Justice League of America, started in the early 1920s as an arm of the Communist Party, USA. It's notable for still being in existence nearly twenty years after the end of the Cold War.

YOUNG COMMUNIST LEAGUE, USA
MEMBERSHIP CARD

YCL Name **Billy Geerh P 4**
Date **MAY 11**

YCL Chapter _____

FIGHT FOR
YOUR FUTURE!

Contact the YCL National Office
235 West 23rd St. NYC, NY 10011 212. 741. 2016
ycl@yclusa.org   www.yclusa.org

5-5-2000

5-5-2000
Dear Billy,

Thank you for joining the Young Communist League, USA. Normally, we limit our membership to young people between the ages of 14 and 30. Because of your early commitment to the socialist cause, though, we're giving you an "honorary" membership from now until you turn 14, at which time you'll become a full member.

I hope you'll be able to take part in some of the activities coming up in the LA area this summer, and become an active YCLer! (I'll be sending you more information about summer YCL stuff later.)

In Solidarity,
Jen Barnett
National Membership Coordinator
YCL USA
P.S. Sorry it took so long to get this to you!

Dear Billy,

Thank you for joining the Young Communist League, USA. Normally, we limit our membership to young people between the ages of 14 and 30. Because of your early commitment to the socialist cause, though, we're giving you an "honorary" membership from now until you turn 14, at which time you'll become a full member.

I hope you'll be able to take part in some of the activities coming up in the LA area this summer, and become an active YCLer! (I'll be sending you more iformation about summer YCL stuff later.)

In Solidarity,

Jen Barnett

Jen Barnett
National Membership Coordinator
YCL USA

P.S. –
Sorry it took so long to get this to you.

December 4, 1998

Dear Mr. Lamb,
This is a project for school. We
are supposed to write to someone
We admire and ask a question.
My Dad said you used to be a.
D.J. I am a D.J. for my school's
lunch room. Could you send me a
picture from when you played
music?! Please sign it

⇒

ROCK ON.

Thanks,
Billy Geerhart

Brian Lamb (C-SPAN)

Whether dealing with foul-mouthed crank callers or prestigious heads of state, C-SPAN's Brian
Lamb always manages to exhibit the same level of unflappable, nonpartisan calm. Lamb, who
is almost certainly half-Vulcan, founded the nonprofit public-affairs cable channel in 1979 and
has been its most visible on-air face ever since. One of the Indiana native's earliest and most
improbable broadcasting gigs was hosting the *American Bandstand*–type show, *Dance Date*.
Perhaps it was his exposure to Fabian-crazed teens on this program that taught the young Lamb
the pitfalls of unchecked emotion.

Dear Billy,

Please find enclosed your requested photo. I'm sorry that it took us so long to get it to you. It actually took us a while to find Brian's "Dance Date" photos!

Many thanks for your kind letter, and best of luck to you in the upcoming school year.

All the best,
Lea Anne Fong
C-SPAN

400 North Capitol St. NW
Suite 650
Washington, DC 20001
TEL. 202. 737. 3220

Dear Billy,

Please find enclosed your requested photo. I'm sorry that it took us so long to get it to you. It actually took us a while to find Brian's "Dance Date" photos!

Many thanks for your kind letter, and best of luck to you in the upcoming school year.
All the best,
Lea Anne Fong
C-SPAN

To Billy — "Rock On" from Brian P. Lamb (former Dance Date Host)

BRIAN LAMB (C-SPAN)   205

April 7, 1999

Dear Mr. O'Grady,

I have a bet with my friend
Eddie that I can eat 100 worms.
My brother said You'd be a good
person to ask advise oh how to
eat allot of bugs. Could You give
some pointers? Should I boil
the worms first. Please allso
send a picture.

Thank You!

Billy

Scott O'Grady

The U.S. Air Force F-16 pilot became momentarily famous when he was shot down over Bosnia in 1995 and eluded capture for six days while surviving on leaves, grass, and ants. O'Grady was rescued by the Marines and soon thereafter returned to the United States for a hero's welcome. The courageous flier even attended a White House lunch with President Bill Clinton during which he politely declined the first course, which may have borne too much of a resemblance to his recent survival diet. The *New York Times* quoted O'Grady as saying "Excuse me, Mr. President, if I don't eat my salad."

June 1, 1999

Billy Geerhart

Dear Billy,

I am in receipt of your letter concerning your bet with your friend Eddie.

I would not recommend eating 100 worms. I would not recommend eating 100 of anything. Before I ate the ants, I had taken a survival training course which helped us know what plants or insects were safe. You don't ever knowingly want to do something that could be harmful to you or your body.

I am glad you liked my book Basher Five-Two. I wrote that book especially for young readers like you. In the Air Force, we are trained to fly safe and to take care of ourselves and our buddies. So you be sure to take good care of y-o-u and your friend Eddie.

Keep up the good work in school and remember, whether riding in a car or a plane, always wear your seat belt.

Have a fun - and safe summer.

GOD Bless
Scott O'Grady

GOD Bless
Scott O'Grady

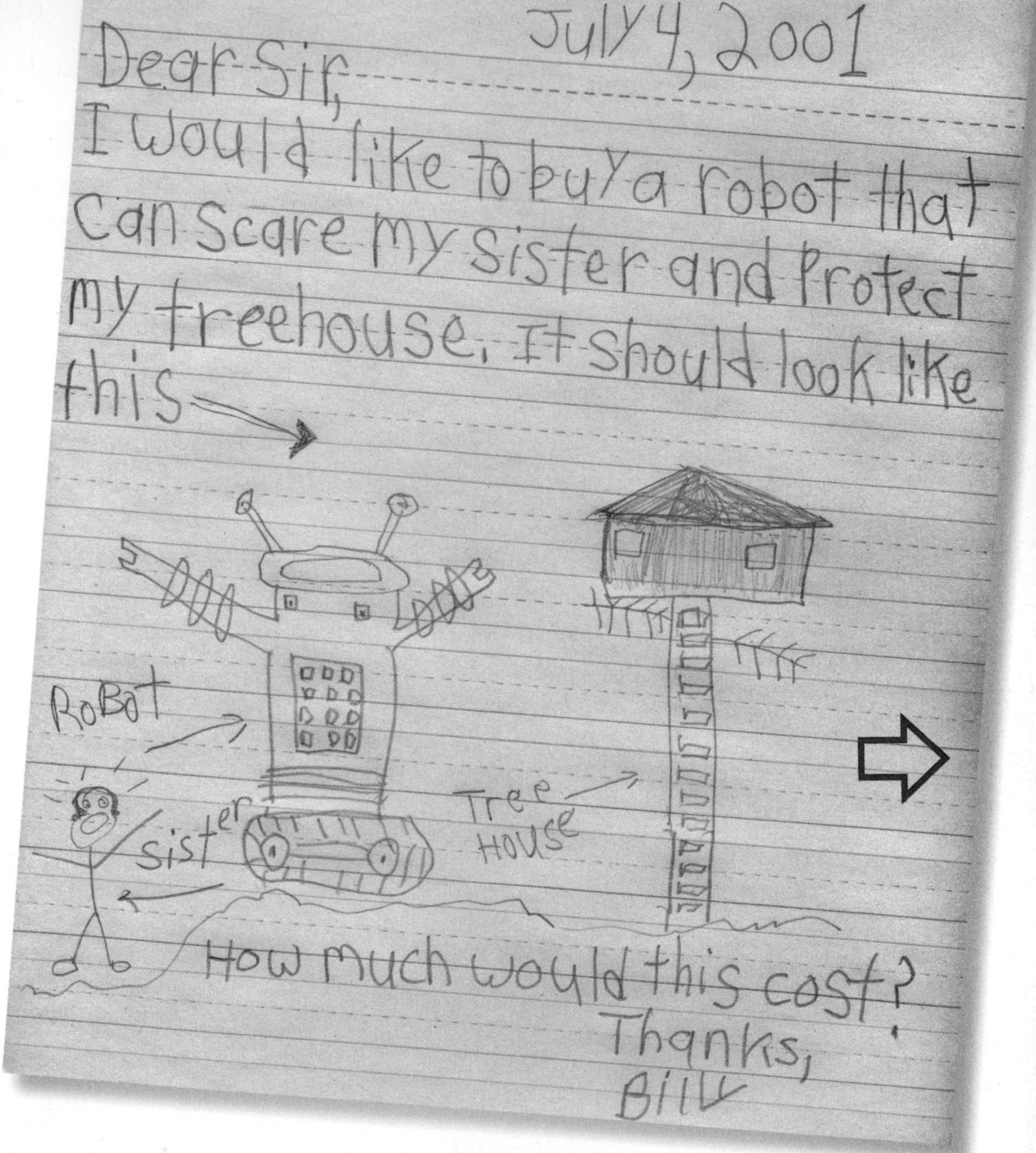

Handwritten letter:

July 4, 2001

Dear Sir,
I would like to buy a robot that can scare my sister and protect my treehouse. It should look like this →

Robot →

Sister

Tree House →

How much would this cost?
Thanks,
Bill

American Robot Corporation

This Pittsburgh, Pennsylvania–based firm specializes in producing robotics for the military and aerospace markets. From a quick review of the business's website, it appears that they have yet to manufacture a robot that is capable of scaring a five-year-old girl.

July 17, 2001

Dear Billy,

Hello! My name is Caitlin, and I'm the daughter of Peyton Collins, the owner of American Robot. I also work at American Robot sometimes. My father really enjoyed your letter. You're an excellent artist!

As for the robot you had in mind, we don't make kinds like that but maybe we'll start to. See Billy, I think you're talented enough to make your own scary robot to protect your tree house and scare your sister. Ask your mom or dad to help you build one. You could use cardboard, markers, and many other things you can find around the house.

If you have the time, I'd love to hear →

With apologies to Mr. Manson, this is probably the most creative reply Little Billy has ever received.

more from you. How old are you? What kind of things do you like to do? What's your favorite TV show?

If you get the chance, write back. You can also ask any more questions you may have about robots. Use this address:

Caitlin Collins

Have a terrific day!

Sincerely,
Caitlin
(representing American
Robot Corporation)

Dear Sir,

July 4, 2001

I would like to buy a robot that can scare my sister and protect my treehouse. It should look like this?

Robot →

← Sister

Treehouse

How much would this cost? Please write me back.

Thanks,
Billy

CRS Robotics

This very successful robotics company is based in Canada and played a role in the historic Human Genome Project. The business now has its own Wikipedia entry and videos of their robot models performing, well, robotically on YouTube.

CRS *It's all about time*

July 19, 2001

CRS ROBOTICS CORPORATION
5344 JOHN LUCAS DRIVE,
BURLINGTON, ONTARIO
CANADA L7L 6A6

TEL (905) 332 2000
FAX (905) 332 1114

TOLL FREE 1 800 365 7587
EMAIL info@crsrobotics.com
WEB www.crsrobotics.com

Billy Geerhart
USA

Dear Master Geerhart:

Thank you for taking the time to write to us and inquire about CRS Robotics' robots.

We manufacture different robot types for various applications to help companies improve their work tasks. Perhaps a better way than to use one of our robots to scare your sister away from your treehouse, would be to send an invitation to your sister outlining certain times you would not mind her visiting you in your treehouse. This way your sister can feel special that you are including her and you can control how often your sister is allowed to visit your treehouse.

I am enclosing an information package, including specifics on our robots. Thank you again for your interest in our company.

Sincerely,

Mike Peerenboom
North American Sales Manager
Laboratory Automation

Enclosure

/gg

Little Billy did give these guys permission to use the drawing on their trade-show T-shirts, but made them promise that his dad would get an XXL for free. We never got the shirt, which really sucks! Maybe somebody should update their Wikipedia page so everybody will know about this!

CRS *It's all about time*

Jan.22, 2002

Billy Geerhart

Dear Master Geerhart,

We are writing to ask your permission to use the letter that you sent us last July. We would like to transfer your letter unto t-shirts to be given away at an upcoming tradeshow. We will not be selling these shirts. We are impressed with your creativity and we would like to share it with others. With your permission, we can proceed with this idea. Of course, we would like to send you a few shirts for you and your family. We have been unable to locate a phone number for you and that is why we are sending this request via Fed-x. Please call me, Mike Peerenboom, at (714)-273-8439 at your earliest convenience with your decision. Thank you for your consideration.

Sincerely,

Mike Peerenboom
North American Sales Manager
Laboratory Automation

April 8, 1999

Dear Govenor Bush,

This is a project for school. We are supposed to write to the candidates and ask a question. My question is what is your plan for an alien invasion of the earth? Could you allso send me a picture?

Thank you,
Billy

George W. Bush

In retrospect, Bush's form letter nonresponse to Billy's question about the then-candidate's plan for a possible space alien invasion offers an intriguing preview of the level of attention that the new administration would give to documents concerning national security.

Governor
George W. Bush
PRESIDENTIAL EXPLORATORY COMMITTEE, INC.

April 12, 1999

This was back before W.

cared about evildoers

(like invading space aliens).

Mr. Billy Geerhart

Dear Billy,

Thank you for your thoughtful letter. I am deeply grateful for your support. Because young people are so important to me and to the future of Texas and the United States, I have made education my number one priority.

Your education is your most important job right now. I encourage you to study hard, set high goals and work hard to achieve them. With determination and focus, you can build a successful future.

I also encourage you to do your part to make America a better place to live. There are many things young people can do to improve our nation. One of the best ways to make a difference is to volunteer, giving your time and talents to a neighbor, your church, a charity or a community organization. I urge you to work for a more caring society.

Best wishes in your studies, and have a good school year.

Sincerely,

George W. Bush

George W. Bush

Post Office Box 1902, Austin Texas 78767-1902
OFFICE: 512-637-2000 **FAX:** 512-637-8800 www.georgewbush.com

Paid for by Governor George W. Bush Presidential Exploratory Committee, Inc.

GEORGE W. BUSH **213**

April 8, 1999

Dear Mr. Kasich,
This is a project for my school,
We are supposed to write to a
candidate and ask a question. My
question is what is Your plan in
case of an alien invasion of the
earth? Could You also send me a
picture?

Thank You and
Good Luck,
Billy

➡️

John Kasich

The boyish-looking, genial, eight-term Republican congressman from Ohio was a candidate for president in 2000 before dropping out to endorse George W. Bush. Currently Kasich is a Fox News guest host and contributor. He began his political career as an aide to Donald "Buzz" Lukens, the Ohio Republican congressman who was convicted in 1989 of having sex with a minor. Kasich has written two patriotic feel-good tomes, *Courage Is Contagious* and *Stand for Something: The Battle for America's Soul.*

Kasich 2000

2021 East Dublin-Granville Road
Suite 2000
Columbus, OH 43229
(614) 785-1600
Fax 785-1611

April 22, 1999

Billy Geerhart

Dear Billy:

Thank you for taking the time to write to me. I always enjoy corresponding with young people. I hope I am able to help you with your school project.

In your letter, you ask about the nation's defense against an alien invasion. While our government has historically researched the possibility of extraterrestrial life, there has been little evidence to support such a defense system. The main purpose of our national defense is to protect against invasions from other countries.

You may be interested to learn about the Search for Extraterrestrial Intelligence (SETI) project. SETI began as a private research project. In the 1970s, the National Aeronautics and Space Administration (NASA) took interest in the project, agreed to fund it, and renamed it the Towards Other Planetary Systems/High Resolution Microwave Survey (TOPS/HRMS) program.

NASA no longer funds this program, however, you may be interested to know the SETI program currently receives private donations which enable it to continue the work conducted at NASA. If you would like more information, contact SETI Institute, 2035 Landings Dr., Mountain View, CA 94043.

Once again, thank you for writing. Like you, I am intrigued by space science and I believe we need to utilize and develop space. I support the development of space as long as we undertake such goals in a science-driven manner and a balanced budget framework. I wish you all the best on your school project.

Sincerely,

John R. Kasich
Representative to Congress

JRK/jc

Dear Mr. Alexander,
This is a project for my school.
We are supposed to write to the
canditates and ask a question. My
Questions is what is your plan in
case of an alien invasion of the
earth? Could you also send me
a picture?

Good Luck!
Billy

Lamar Alexander

The plaid-loving former governor of Tennessee and secretary of education under George H. W. Bush was a two-time failed Republican presidential candidate before becoming a senator in 2003. The bland Alexander's one nonwonkish quality (besides his fondness for plaid) is his talent for playing country-music piano. In 2007 the senator tickled the ivories on Patti Page's rerecording of her 1950s hit *Tennessee Waltz*.

ALEXANDER
P R E S I D E N T

Campaign Headquarters
2000 Glen Echo Road, Suite 207   Nashville, Tennessee 37215
615/ 620-2000   *fax* 615/ 620-2001

Finance Office
2000 Glen Echo Road, Suite 107   Nashville, Tennessee 37215
615/ 620-2030   *fax* 615/ 620-2031

April 14, 1999

Master Billy Geerhart

Dear Billy:

I have signed the photograph, as you requested, which is much easier than your question.

Here is my plan in case of an alien invasion of the earth. I would immediately take all of the aliens to Washington, D.C. where they would become so confused that they would promptly return to wherever they came from.

Thanks for writing. Very best wishes.

Sincerely,

Lamar Alexander

website: www.lamaralexander.com   Paid for by Alexander for President, Inc.
                                 Contributions are not deductible for federal income tax purposes.

email: info@lamaralexander.com

Dear Ms. Stouffer,
This is a project for my school.
We are supposed to write to a public
person and ask a question. My
Dad watches Headline News <u>all</u> the
time. I was wondering if you
could add cartoons at the end of
the half hour for kids like me?
What do you think of this idea? I am
writing other people at your channel
for extra credit. Could you also send
me a picture?   Thank You,
                                 Billy Geerhart

CNN Headline News

Headline News was originally launched in 1982 as "CNN2," a companion network to the
CNN 24-hour news channel. Its format was a segmented, rotating approach to news reporting
(major headlines, financial news, sports, entertainment). Linda Stouffer's response to Billy is
prescient because, beginning in 2005, Headline News changed its format to make room for
human cartoons Nancy Grace and Glenn Beck, and the anchor, in fact, did find herself "out of
a job" in 2008.

Billy,
Thank you for your letter.
I am glad you picked me for
your school project and hope
you get a good grade.
I will give your cartoon idea
to my Executive Producer to
see what he thinks. However,
if we start running cartoons I
might be out of a job!
—Linda

Billy,
Thank you for your letter. I am glad you
picked me for your school project and hope
you get a good grade.
I will give your cartoon idea to my
Executive Producer to see what he thinks.
However, if we start running cartoons, I
might be out of a job!

—Linda

A Time Warner Company

LINDA STOUFFER

october 14, 2008

Dear Govenor Palin,

This is a project for my school, We're supposed to write to someone public we admire and ask a question. My Grampa helped me find your adress. He likes the way you wink at him from the T.V. My question is if my family visted Alaska would you take us wolf hunting from your helicopter? That would really be cool! Could you allso send a picture?

Sincerely,
Billy

Governor Sarah Palin

The 1984 Miss Alaska runner-up, moose dresser, and governor of Alaska was the first woman to be nominated for vice president by the Republican Party. Palin and her quirky Wasilla-isms exploded onto the national scene when Senator John McCain shocked the world by choosing her as his running mate in 2008. After a stunning debut that briefly elevated her ticket mate's poll numbers, the governor quickly proved herself to be the least qualified major party candidate since Dan Quayle. Highlights of her ill-fated campaign include an ABC News interview in which she links her foreign-policy expertise to her state's proximity to Russia (later satirically distilled to the phrase "I can see Russia from my house!" by comedian Tina Fey); a CBS News interview in which she appears to be stumped by a question about what newspapers she reads; and falling prey (for six minutes!) to a prank call from a radio shock jock pretending to be the president of France. In 2009 Palin floored the political establishment by resigning her office midterm.

Billy—
Thank you for your letter to Governor Palin. I'll get it to her tomorrow. Like your Grandpa, I also like the way Sarah winks.

I'm helping her with her mail now as she's receiving hundreds of letters weekly and her family has to help her to keep up.

No wolf hunting from helicopters here. The news media thought that up. It is done in Russia though where pictures came from

Best Regards,
Chuck Heath
Sarah's dad

Little Billy was touched that Governor Palin and her dad share an irrational distrust of the media. It must be hereditary.

November 16, 1998

Dear Gloria,
This is a project for my 3rd grade class. We are supposed to write someone and ask a question. I was wondering if the Six Million Man hit the Bionic Woman in a fight would that be wrong? My brother says it would be a fair fight. My teacher helped me find your address.
Thank you very much,
Billy Geerhart

Gloria Steinem

An icon of American feminism, Steinem began her professional life as a journalist publishing groundbreaking articles such as a 1962 piece on the birth control pill in *Esquire* and a 1963 feature for *Show* magazine that recounted her undercover experiences as a Playboy Bunny. In 1972 she cofounded *Ms.* magazine, a publication that still bears her name on the masthead. After the Clarence Thomas Supreme Court confirmation battle, Steinem mused in a speech attended by Thomas's sexual-harassment accuser Anita Hill how the porn-loving justice might be impeached and replaced by Hill someday. In 2000 Steinem married the environmentalist and animal rights activist David Bale, father of the actor Christian Bale. David Bale passed away in 2003.

Gloria Steinem

2 December 1998

Billy Geerhart

Dear Billy,

Thanks for your note to Gloria Steinem and for thinking of her for your project. In response to your question—"if the Six Million Dollar Man hit the Bionic Woman in a fight would that be wrong"— the short answer to your question is yes. As Gloria explained to me, it would only be fair if it was done in self-defense.

Good luck with your project.

Sincerely,

Amy Richards.

Amy Richards

Little Billy regrets that he forgot to ask Ms. Steinem about fembots.

Bill,

Greetings. Received your letter. Glad to hear my letter to you in 99 made a difference. When do you graduate? Yeah get me a subscription to Radar magazine. What is it about? Know any asian girls willing to correspond? Send pictures. You can photocopy 5 on 1 page or send em singular. Nothing scenic though. Send some of girls in bikinis. Do you go clubbing? Seen any good movies? Saw '3:10 to Yuma' the other day. It was an OK western. Didn't do too good at the box office though. Do you have family? I'm the youngest of five. That's all for now. Take it E/Z write when you get a chance.
Your friend
Richard

Richard Ramirez, E37101
San Quentin Prison
San Quentin, CA 94964

January 18, 2008

Dear Mr. Ramirez,

Thanks to your wise, succinct advice back in 1999, I decided to stay in school and today I am studying law at a prestigious university. This is just a letter of thanks.

By the way, I noticed on your LostVault.com Pen Pal ad that you have a good sense of humor. Do you ever read Radar magazine? It is hilarious. Let me know. I'd like to get you a subscription if you want one. Or are you more a Mad Magazine kind of guy?

Best,
Bill Geerhart

Richard Ramirez, aka the Night Stalker (2008)

What can one say about the Night Stalker that hasn't already been said? Not much aside from the fact that since his first letter, he apparently ran out of personalized stationery and developed a taste for westerns and Asian women.

Bill,

Greetings. Received your letter. Glad to hear my letter to you in 99 made a difference. When do you graduate? Yeah get me a subscription to Radar magazine. What is it about? Know any asian girls willing to correspond? Send pictures. You can photocopy 5 on 1 page or send em singular. Nothing scenic though. Send some of girls in bikini. Do you go out klubbing? Seen any good movies? Saw '3:10 to yuma' the other day. It was an ok western. Didn't do too good at the box office though. Do you have family? I'm the youngest of five. Thats all for now. Take it E/Z write when you get a chance.

Your friend

R.

Charles Manson, B-33920
4A 4R-23
P. O. Box 3476
Corcoran, CA 93212

December 22, 2007

Dear Mr. Manson,

This is a belated letter of thanks. You probably do not recall, but back in 1998 I wrote you a letter seeking advice on whether or not to drop out of elementary school (see attached). Your wise counsel persuaded me to continue with my education and today I am an undergraduate at Harvard University. I am at home for the winter break and I came across your letter today while going through some of my papers. It occurred to me at this time just how much I owe you.

Thanks to your timely response to my letter nine years ago, I am now well on my way to realizing my dream of getting my college degree and then going on to law school (my goal is to eventually become a prosecutor).

I bet you never realized that you had that kind of influence on people, did you?

I could go on and on, but I think I should probably just leave it at "thanks."

There is, however, one question that I have for you: what was the deal with the photo of that shack that you sent along with your letter back in '98? I've often pondered its significance.

I look forward to hearing back from you. Thanks again for helping me find my path.

Kindest Regards and Happy Holidays,

Bill Geerhart

Charles Manson (2008)

Strangely enough, Manson really opens up in this second letter, but ten years later he's still not ready to explain the significance of that creepy barn photo. . . .

Charles Manson
B-33920
4A 4R 3
PO Box 3476
Corcoran, CA 93212

BAKERSFIELD CA 933
MOJAVE CA
07 JAN 2008 PM 3 T

HAPPY
HOLI...

USA 41

STATE
PRISON
CORCORAN

BILL Geerhart

9001241553 C002

The smiley face was just the tip of
the iceberg for this letter....

You even typing now—cool—A Hillbilly that can typ—far out.

I know if you payed what you owe you would be brok brok in like broak ones a panter brock + that they is a crook

LETTER PROPER:

Hay Lo Soul Good To Too Two 2 here from you. I thought things got so good for you that you just 4 Got what you could of remembered or could remember what you don't forgit. Where is your mind—must you watch TV all day + go to night school to be a D.A.? JUST to forgit I didn't take your money when I had ALL your credit cards locked up in

The [illegible] turns—code 3.

my dreams—Rife with Con Va Lution due 2 subjewgashen. My spelling got better— see when you go to school you learn to spell— oh well I'm JUST playing clown words to say I didn't forgit Hellbilly— Bill we always had good days + Im glad your gonna be a D.A. Be one who works for justice + not one who just wants to WIN WIN + and don't care if people didn't do Rong— anyway be as good as you are when you git a JOB + dont let the job make you bad you make the JOB good. Easy Charles Manson

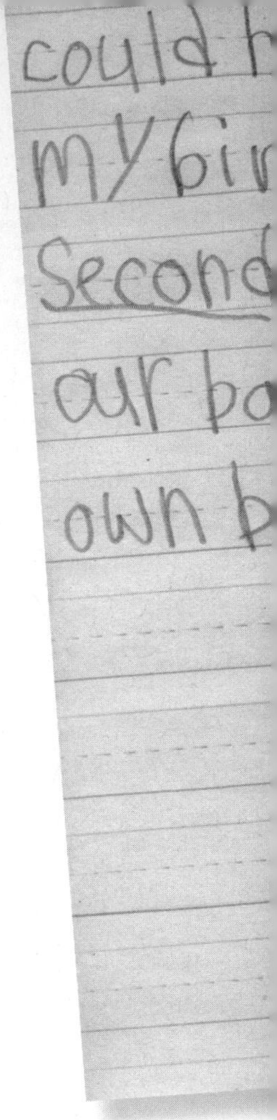

could h
my bir
Second
our ba
own b

ve the Olson twins come

hday party on August 26?

choice A swimming

k

dro

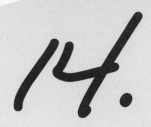

[Dead Letter Department]

march 29, 1999

Dear Mr. Rushdie,
My friend Eddie said you were
good at hiding. If I were to run
away from home could you give
some pointers on hiding? Please
also send me a picture.

Thank you,
Billy Geerhart

*My dad told me that the people
in this chapter may have been too
busy to write back to me. And, no,
my dad didn't have any idea what
would be taking up so much of
    J. D. Salinger's time.*

Salman Rushdie

The Indian-born British author wrote the 1988 book *The Satanic Verses*, which caused a firestorm of controversy in the Muslim world because of its depiction of the prophet Muhammad and other Islamic figures. In 1989 Iran's Ayatollah Ruhollah Khomeini issued a fatwa—or religious edict—calling for Rushdie's execution. As a result, Rushdie went underground for most of the next decade surfacing only occasionally to hang out with U2 or to deliver a Top Ten list to David Letterman. Even though religious authorities in Iran continue to assert the validity of the fatwa, Rushdie has resumed his public life, but sadly divorced from his model wife, Padma.

march 29, 1999
History
Third Grade

Dear Sen. Thurmond,
This is a project for my school. We
are doing a unit on Black History and
we are allowed to write to a public official
for extra credit. I wanted to ask You
what it was like to own slaves. What
were Your slaves names? How many did
You own? Could You also send me a picture
of You with Your slaves?

Thank You,
Billy Geerhart

Strom Thurmond

This failed segregationist, Dixiecrat candidate for president in 1952 was a long-serving senator from South Carolina. Thurmond, who was a Democrat until switching parties to become a Republican in 1964, made his mark on the Senate when he attempted to derail the Civil Rights Act of 1957 with the longest one-man filibuster in American history. The indefatigably racist lawmaker speechified for an astounding 24 hours and 18 minutes. The bill passed anyway, sixty-two to fifteen. Thurmond, who is the only senator to reach the age of one hundred while in office, retired in 2003 and passed away six months later. Shortly after his death it was revealed that as a young man Thurmond had fathered a child with a sixteen-year-old African American family servant. While the senator never openly acknowledged his mixed-race daughter, he did support her financially into adulthood.

April 17, 1999

Dear Mr. Salinger,

My mom and I are big fans of yours and love your books.

But my mom says you very sick and need a new kidny fast. I just wanted to let you know you can have one of mine if you want. I hope you feel better, could you send me a picture when you write back?

Thank you,
BILLY

J. D. Salinger

Salinger is the recluse author of the disturbed loner classic *Catcher in the Rye*. Even though the New Hampshire–based literary icon hasn't published a word (outside of lawsuits) in nearly half a century, he is still the object of obsession by liberal arts majors and depressed teens. In 1987 it was revealed that the writer had an obsession of his own: *Dynasty* star Catherine Oxenberg. He reportedly fell in love with the nighttime soap star from watching her on television and even traveled to Los Angeles to meet her. His unhinged quest was cut short when he was allegedly escorted off of the TV show's soundstage like an aging Holden Caulfield.

July 2, 2000

Dear Make a Wish,

My friend Eddie says you guys grant wishes. I was wondering if you could have the Olson Twins come to my birthday party on August 26? Second choice <u>A</u> swimming pool for our back yard. Third choice my own bedroom.

Thanks,

Billy

*Eddie didn't mention anything
about having to be sick.*

Make-A-Wish Foundation

A nonprofit organization that was founded in 1980 to grant wishes to children with "life-threatening medical conditions."

December 1, 1998

Dear O, J,
my whole family thinks you are guilty but I do not, I want to help you find the real killers and I am sending you my allowance, I hope it helps,

Little Billy wants his allowance money back!

I am also running for ~~class~~ grade ~~to~~ ~~with~~ ~~ele~~

Thank you,
Billy Geerhart

O. J. Simpson

The football star, B-movie actor, and acquitted double-murder defendant had to suspend his search for the "real killers" in 2008 because he was sentenced to thirty-three years in prison for a comically inept Las Vegas sports-memorabilia robbery. Simpson, who once tried to profit from the murders of his ex-wife and her friend in a hypothetical confessional entitled *If I Did It*, is currently reaping what is hopefully but a small, karmic down payment in the Lovelock Correctional Center in Nevada.

May 12, 1999

Dear O.D.B.,
This is a project for school.
for extra credit we can write to
anyone want to in the arts and ask
a question. I want to be a rapper but
I need a cool name like yours.
could you give some ideas?
could you allso send me a
picture?

Thank You,
Billy

Ol' Dirty Bastard (ODB)

This American rap and hip-hop artist was one of the founding members of the Wu-Tang Clan. Russell Tyrone Jones derived his stage name from the 1980 kung fu film *Ol' Dirty and the Bastard*. He memorably interrupted the 1998 Grammy Awards with a bizarre rant about his wardrobe. ODB embarked on a successful solo career in 1995, but he also had various run-ins with the law resulting from his drug use. He died from an overdose at the age of thirty-five in 2004.

[ACKNOWLEDGMENTS]

This book would not exist if Adam Laukhuf had not found these letters funny enough to excerpt in the late, great *Radar* magazine back in 2008. It was the exposure in *Radar* that eventually led to this deluxe collection you now hold in your hands, and I am forever grateful to Adam for taking a chance on me. Lauren Ambramo, my agent from Dystel & Goderich Literary Management, is another person who took a gamble by signing me as a client, and I hope she still thinks that was a sound decision. Lauren is quite simply the best. Matthew Benjamin is my extremely gifted editor who recognized these letters as being worthy of a book and somehow managed to convince management at HarperCollins to go along with the idea. I am still amazed. Mere words cannot adequately convey my gratitude to Matthew; his editorial assistant, Jessica Deputato; designer, Richard Oriolo; my publicist, Christine Maddalena; and everyone else at HarperCollins for making this book such a stunning reality. The author and the publisher also wish to thank The Topps Company, Inc., for their permission to reproduce the cards contained in this book.

If the reader will grant an indulgence, I'd also like to take this opportunity to honor Humphry Berkeley who more or less got the whole hoax letter genre started in England back in the 1940s with his hilarious Rochester Sneath correspondence (though it wasn't actually published until the 1970s). And the incomparable Don Novello, of course, popularized the form in the United States as Lazlo Toth in his series of *Lazlo Letter* books—still the universal gold standard of prank correspondence. Billy and I owe a significant inspirational debt to these two fine gentlemen of letters.

And, finally, some random but heartfelt thanks to family, friends, enablers, and cherished institutions: the entire Geerhart family (Mom, Dad, Chuck, Cathy, Con, and my amazing Aunt Lil), my old roommate and pal Scott Rodgers (especially for putting up with all of those strange visits from the Mormons), Veronica Lane (Scott's lovely bride), the prank auteur Alan Abel, David Cross, Larry Gelbart, John Riddle, Ken Sitz, Teresa Piccolotti, Elliott Sitz, Jayne Loader, Jack Gantos, Linda Kyriazi, Royce Reed and Marilyn Hoggatt, John Goldsmith, Tim Goldsmith, Elizabeth Molin (for introducing me to the wonders of Lazlo Toth), Franklin Molin, Richard Weize, Brigit Niels, Michael Ravnitzky, Rich Turiel, Faith Williams, Curtis Samson, Michele Nelson, Ethan Samson, Rob "Mondo" Schaffner, Jay McKibben, David Stenn, Phillipa Fallon, Christine Mustizer, Michael J. Weldon and *Psychotronic Video*, Bear Family Records, *Spy* magazine, and, last but not least, Xenu.

Bill Geerhart is the cofounder of the Cold War popular-culture website CONELRAD.com and is a producer for the vintage country and rock label Bear Family Records. His writing has appeared in *Radar*, the *Bulletin of the Atomic Scientists*, and Adult Christianity. Bill lives in Los Angeles, where aberrant behavior is encouraged and frequently rewarded.